THE ULTIMATE
SUPERHERO
MOVIE GUIDE

THIS IS A CARLTON BOOK

Published by Carlton Books Ltd
20 Mortimer Street
London W1T 3JW

ISBN 978-1-78739-260-1

Editor: Ross Hamilton
Design: Russell Knowles, James Pople
Production: Rachel Burgess

A CIP catalogue for this book is available from the British Library

10 9 8 7 6 5 4 3 2 1

Printed in Dubai

THE ULTIMATE
SUPERHERO
MOVIE GUIDE

THE DEFINITIVE HANDBOOK FOR
COMIC BOOK FILM FANS

HELEN O'HARA

CARLTON
BOOKS

CONTENTS

INTRODUCTION

ARE COMIC-BOOK SUPERHEROES A NEW MYTHOLOGY THROUGH WHICH WE EXAMINE OR ESCAPE THE MODERN WORLD? OR ARE THEY CARTOONISH VISIONS OF GOOD AND EVIL FOR PEOPLE WHO HAVE FAILED TO GROW UP? IF YOU HAVE PICKED UP THIS BOOK, YOU'RE PROBABLY IN THE FORMER CAMP, AND FOR MY MONEY IT'S THE CORRECT ONE. COMIC BOOKS ARE NO LONGER JUST FOR KIDS, AND SUPERHEROES ARE NO LONGER JUST FOR COMICS.

Look at the sheer variation on offer in the comic-book superheroes we've seen onscreen. They can be dark, twisted and deeply compromised in their morality; they can lack powers entirely if they train hard and/or have a butler called Alfred; they can tell twisting, intricate tales over years at a time and 22 consecutive films (and counting). Like them or not, they are a cinema fixture in the 2000s and likely to remain so as long as filmmakers can find fresh stories and new ways to make us relate to even indestructible aliens. They're characters we love, often (not always) embodying moral examples that we can aspire to, and they're a heck of a lot better looking than the rest of us. Well, mostly. Sorry, Deadpool.

In trying to round up the biggest and best comic-book superhero movies, I've had to make some tough choices. The focus, first of all, is on Hollywood superhero movies. They have conquered the world almost unopposed by the efforts of Japanese anime, big-budget Bollywood or anyone else. This is not to say that those films aren't good – just that this is almost a separate genre from the output of other countries.

Then I narrowed the criteria to films based on comics, which knocked out a surprising number of hits, from *The Incredibles* to *Darkman* (those are rounded up on page 164). Finally, I weighed the rest by superheroism, so I judged *Jonah Hex* too mystical-Western and *300* super-heroic only in its personal training regime. *Constantine* squeaked in because he acts like a superhero, even if he's technically a warlock. *Batman* gets a pass despite his lack of powers, because Batman always does. Rich people, eh?

Before you ask, the superhero requirement knocks out many incredible comic-book adaptations, such as *A History of Violence*, *Road to Perdition*, *Ghost World*, *Persepolis* and *The Death of Stalin*. I highly recommend checking those out if you haven't already, and exploring the wider world of non-superhero comics.

I'm sure I'll be accused of favouritism in my choices, so I'll cop to it immediately. The films I think are best get most space here, and in recent years that includes more Marvel films than DC. In the great battle between the two comic-book titans, I am Team Marvel despite my fondness for Superman, Wonder Woman and the rest. However, I've tried to bunch Marvel's prolific output by sub-franchises or we'd be here all day, and the single most-featured character is Batman, so I hope you'll forgive me for liking Captain America better.

These films aren't perfect; some of my favourites aren't even that great (hello, *Tank Girl*). But as a whole they are inspiring. In this cynical, compromised and sometimes horrifying world, it's encouraging to see people who stand up for the little guy and try to stop evil – not because it's their job but because they simply want to help. The same capacity is in all of us, and they remind us of it. So watching and researching all these films over again has been a positively inspiring experience. I could do this all day.

Helen O'Hara, 2019

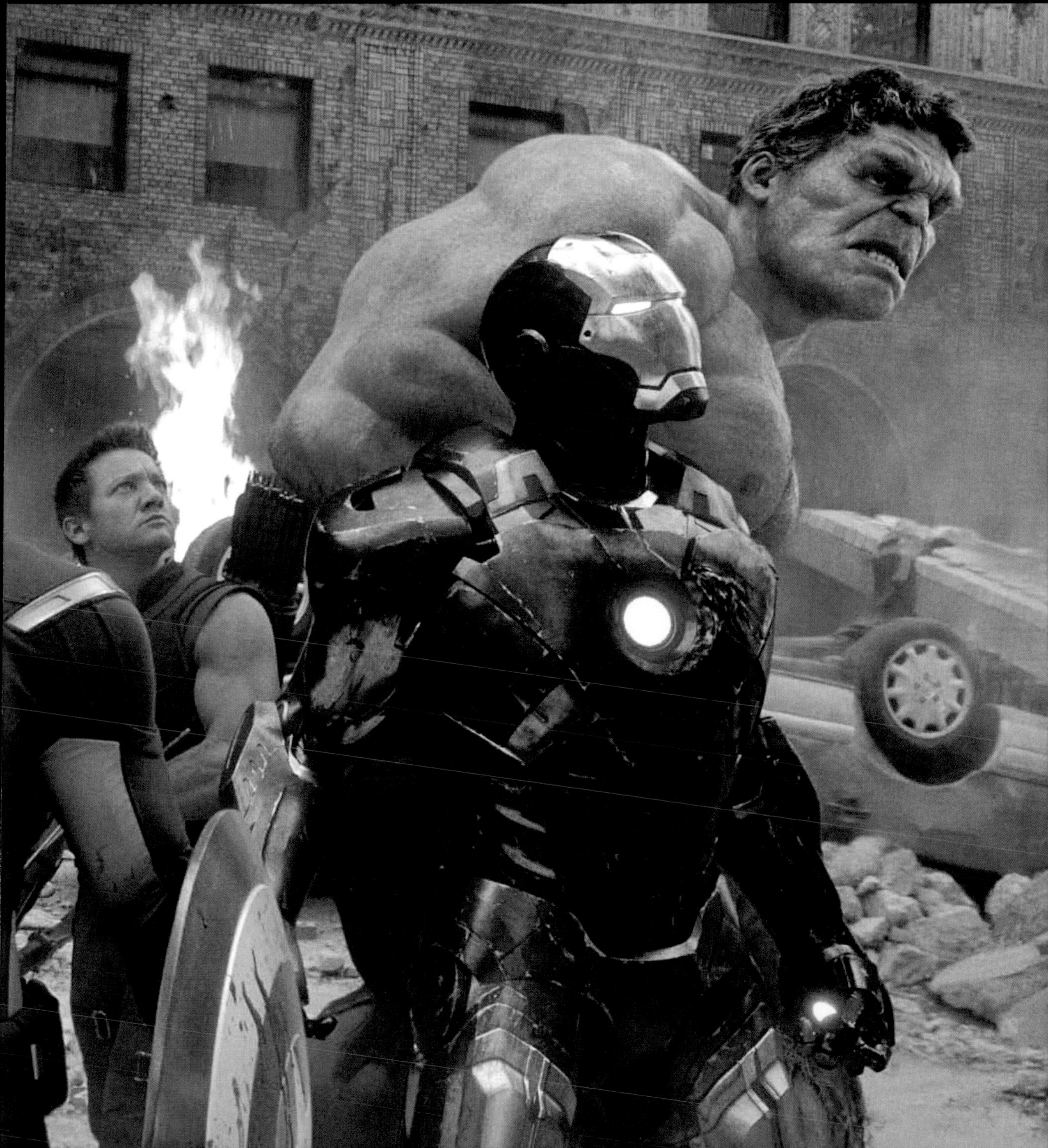

SUPERMAN AND SUPERMAN II

SUPERMAN IS SORT OF MIRACULOUS. THIS FIRST MAJOR SUPERHERO FILM SET THE BAR SO HIGH THAT ABOUT HALF THE FILMS SINCE HAVE FAILED TO MATCH IT. THE TAGLINE PROMISED "YOU'LL BELIEVE A MAN CAN FLY", AND WE DID. ALSO, SHOOT RAYS FROM HIS EYES, SEE THROUGH LADIES' DRESSES AND TURN THE WORLD BACK ON ITS AXIS. SCRATCH A MODERN SUPERHERO-MOVIE DIRECTOR AND YOU'LL FIND SOMEONE WHO WATCHED THIS, GOGGLE-EYED AS A KID AND DECIDED TO DO THAT WHEN THEY GREW UP.

The key was that producer Alexander Salkind took the subject seriously. He knew there was gold in them thar hills, but that it would take a vast investment to mine for the superhero-movie motherlode. He put down a then-startling $55-million budget (equivalent to $200 million+ today: these films have always been spendy). That bonanza paid for The Godfather himself, Marlon Brando, to establish the world as Superman's father Jor-El, and *Godfather* author Mario Puzo to write the film's story. It persuaded Gene Hackman to take a break from serious character work to try his hand at a preening, ridiculous and yet deadly Lex Luthor.

There is a little self-consciousness in the pre-credit scene of a comic-book narrated by a young boy. But director Richard Donner and his team quickly settle in, building Superman's history on both Krypton and Earth over nearly an hour (all ten seasons of Smallville take about five minutes). Teen actor Jeff East soon makes way for the one true Superman, Christopher Reeve. On only his second film, Reeve connected absolutely to the character's essential decency. He stayed in character between scenes, despite constant teasing from Margot "Lois Lane" Kidder. Reeve's embrace of the responsibility of being Superman lasted for life and, it seemed, helped when he was tragically paralyzed following a riding accident. The Man of Steel had nothing on the strength of character he showed in later life as a campaigner for research into spinal injuries.

Onscreen, too, Reeve was a bit of a miracle. He could be hilarious, and makes such a profound transformation from the Man of Steel to mild-mannered Clark Kent in his too-big suits that you can believe that the *Daily Planet*'s ace reporter might not consider the possibility that they are the same guy. Reeve's hero claims no super-status; he introduces himself simply as "a friend". His first rescue ("You've got me? Who's got you?!") is glorious, but key to selling it are Reeve's lazy barrel rolls over Metropolis afterward and his crime-stopping spree, including the obligatory cat-in-tree rescue. His flight with Lois, soon after, is so magical that it even survives that awful voice-over bit.

Opposite When you see Reeve in full Superman mode, you'll believe a man can fly

The film was a monster success, and Salkind's insistence that Donner shoot the second film simultaneously seemed prescient. But producer and director fell out when the second film was only three-quarters complete, and replacement director Richard Lester ended up reshooting much of the work that had already been done, dialling up the physical comedy for Clark Kent, Luthor and his henchman Otis (Ned Beatty), and even the new trio of Kryptonian criminals who threatened the planet. Those three, led by Terence Stamp's eerily calm, utterly authoritative General Zod, are – with all respect to Hackman – the best villains in any *Superman* film. They are strong enough to test the Man of Steel's abilities, though they lack his experience on Earth, and are deeply twisted.

Superman II opens as terrorists (including Richard "Uncle Vernon Dudsley" Griffiths) threaten to nuke the Eiffel Tower and Superman must save the day and a too-intrepid Lois. But that aside, it's relatively light in major set-pieces; contrast the Metropolis battle against Zod here with Zack Snyder's orgy of destruction in *Man of Steel*. Then he faces a great moral dilemma when Lois realizes his true identity and they admit they're in love: could he live as a normal human to be with her? Of course, he opts for love – but with the bad luck that dogs the superpowered, that's when this new and overwhelming threat arrives.

Even though Superman has outrageous superpowers on the page, both films rely on powers never displayed

Right Gene Hackman's Lex Luthor, making prison stripes look like Saville Row pinstripes.

Below Terrence Stamp's General Zod and his hench-persons Ursa (Sarah Douglas) and Non (Jack O'Halloran).

before or since in their storytelling. The turning-back-the-planet nonsense that caps the first film is notorious, but the sequel sees him grab and throw his chest symbol: resorting to gadgets is *not* a Superman gambit. At least the end of the first film makes emotional sense – of course he would trash the laws of physics and somehow reverse time (don't tell Neil DeGrasse Tyson) to save the woman he loves – but *Superman II* has no such excuse. Such disregard for the canon has become significantly rarer since the advent of the internet, at least.

Still, it works. It helps to have the greatest superhero theme – sorry, Alan Silvestri; thanks for playing, Danny Elfman and Hans Zimmer – with John Williams perfectly capturing the pomp and glory of Krypton, the almost whimsical good nature of Supes himself and the epic scale of the adventure. That basic message – "They can be a great people, Kal-El, they wish to be. They only lack the light to show the way." – is perfect. Superman shows how we could be. He defends the innocent and protects life, always. He is uncynical, unfailingly honest and optimistic at his core. He is hope.

SUPERMAN III AND SUPERMAN IV: THE QUEST FOR PEACE

Reeve's later Super-films experienced diminishing returns. Richard Lester's third instalment, which gives almost more time to Richard Pryor's computer whizz than to either Clark or Supes, is fun but patchy. As would become traditional in superhero three-quels, Superman goes dark in that film (due to red Kryptonite), becoming selfish and cruel before love saves the day and he reverts to type. But *III*'s failings are a fond memory by the time we get to Sidney J. Furie's *The Quest For Peace*, a howling mess wherein Superman accidentally creates his nemesis when trying to disarm the planet. It makes no sense, introduces a mess of unwanted new characters and suffers from terrible effects.

Below He's here to fight for truth, and justice, and the American way.

BATMAN
AND BATMAN RETURNS

AFTER THE FAILURE OF *SUPERMAN IV: THE QUEST FOR PEACE*, HOLLYWOOD
CONCLUDED THAT THE SUPERHERO WELL HAD RUN DRY. IF SUPERMAN, THE MOST
RECOGNIZABLE CHARACTER IN COMICS, COULD FLOP, WHY TRY ANYONE ELSE? BUT
WARNER BROS AND THEIR DEEP BENCH OF DC CHARACTERS HAD OTHER IDEAS.

A new wave of comics writers, led by Alan Moore and Frank Miller, had popularized a darker and more adult tone in the books – something that had not yet been attempted on the big screen. If, they figured, kids reading comics in the 1950s and 1960s were now adults, why shouldn't they welcome movies that reflected that growth? And so Batman began.

The right director came from an unlikely direction. Tim Burton was then coming off the success of *Pee-Wee's Big Adventure*, of all things, but he chimed with the Gothic style and grimy feel of Gotham City. His animation background gave him the visual flair to bring the comics' wilder flourishes to life, and he promised to translate the twisted darkness of books like *The Killing Joke* to the screen, but not so much that the studio would be saddled with an R-rating.

Opposite Michael Keaton as Tim Burton's Batman, by the redesigned, super-sleek Batmobile.

Below Batman dances with the devil in the pale moonlight as he faces Jack Nicholson's Joker.

Casting would prove trickier. Landing Jack Nicholson as the Joker cost a fortune (fair) but guaranteed a veneer of respectability, as well as being an obviously good fit. But Burton pushed for comedian Michael Keaton as Batman, and that caused more consternation. Had there been an internet at the time, social media would have been ablaze; even without it, there was a passionate write-in campaign against the man still best known as Mr Mom.

Time would, however, prove Burton right. Keaton wasn't the most athletic Batman, but he had presence in the mask and managed a certain rich-kid swagger even when playing up Bruce Wayne's nerdy side. British character actor Michael Gough was cast as Alfred, superstar Kim Basinger would be photo-journalist Vicki Vale, and Jerry Hall and Jack Palance filled out the Joker's side of the story.

Burton futzed with the origins of both Batman and the Joker for dramatic symmetry. As a young hoodlum, Jack Napier kills the Wayne parents. Years later and all unaware, Batman (in shades of the "Red Hood" story) fails to save him from falling into a chemical vat from which he emerges insane and green-haired. There is a certain poetic satisfaction to it, but the hardcore fans were *not* impressed; it's hard to imagine any filmmaker now having such licence or taking such liberties.

Still, it worked and the film was a hit, the fifth highest-grossing film ever at that time. Good news, because that gave Tim Burton the chance to go and make *Edward Scissorhands*, and then to return for, well, *Batman Returns*. That would become a triumphant victory lap of a film and one of the great Christmas movies. Michelle Pfeiffer joined the cast as an impossibly slinky Catwoman, Danny DeVito made a perfectly putrid Penguin and Christopher Walken rounded out an eccentrically evil trio as Max Shreck (no relation to the ogre). It's given a darkly comic twist

Above Keaton may have been best known as a comedian, but he made a surprisingly tough Bat.

Opposite Michelle Pfeiffer's definitive, impossibly slinky Catwoman.

BATMAN FOREVER
AND BATMAN AND ROBIN

Joel Schumacher's first neon-edged, hyper-stylized *Batman Forever* is fun: Val Kilmer makes for a more handsome, more confident Bruce Wayne, and he has worthy adversaries in Jim Carrey's Riddler and Tommy Lee Jones' Two-Face. But then came *Batman and Robin*, still a byword for everything wrong with Hollywood. There was the star with the bloated salary (Schwarzenegger), the inexplicable youth-friendly casting (Alicia Silverstone as Batgirl, visiting from "Oxbridge Academy") and, worst of all, nipples on the Bat-suit. The lingering shame of it has presumably driven George Clooney in every artistically minded decision he has made since, however, so perhaps it turned out for the best. No *Batman and Robin*, no *Good Night and Good Luck*.

by Daniel Waters, the man behind classic high school satire *Heathers*, that gives it a distinctly subversive, kinky feel.

By this point, Burton was able to indulge slightly more in motifs that would become familiar across his filmography: weirdos, outcasts, scary clowns, mutated children's toys. More to the point, he gave endless shade and character to his "freaks" – and through them, illuminates his leading man. So Selina Kyle/Catwoman leads a dual life that reflects Batman's own secret identity, but she's more damaged, less restrained. The Penguin reflects his tragic/rich-boy background but without a parent's love, and Shreck reflects his day job as an industrialist tycoon.

So while it's a generally fair criticism, made often in the Nolan years, that Burton's Bat-films are more about the rogues than the Bat himself, it's not entirely accurate: each bad guy shows us something about Batman himself. Moreover, Catwoman in particular is so mesmeric that it's hard to care. Her doomed flirtation with Bruce Wayne as Selina Kyle, and with Batman as Catwoman, is indelible. It's in one such scene that they realize one another's identities, as he repeats her own line back to her: "Mistletoe can be

deadly if you eat it"; "A kiss can be even deadlier if you mean it."

The critics loved it, but *Batman Returns* was not quite such a smash as its predecessor, so the studio handed the keys of the kingdom to Joel Schumacher for the next two films, while Burton used his success to make idiosyncratic films like *The Nightmare Before Christmas* and *Ed Wood*. The live-action Batman would decline once more, until Nolan revived it. But Burton's films remain a stylish, pleasantly comic-book take on the Dark Knight. They may be more Gothic than realistic, but they look good in black.

BATMAN: MASK OF THE PHANTASM

A NON-NEGLIGIBLE NUMBER OF BAT-FANS CLAIM THAT THE ANIMATED SERIES AND ITS FEATURE FILM SPIN-OFFS PROVIDE THE DEFINITIVE SCREEN BATMANS. WHAT'S MORE, THEY HAVE A PRETTY GOOD CASE.

Each episode of the show generally told a self-contained and surprisingly well-developed story; this feature-length cinema release has a plot that's at least as complex as any live-action effort. And it shows a deep commitment to character, managing a superb job on both Bruce Wayne/Batman (voiced by Kevin Conroy, the longest-standing Batman) and the Joker (Mark Hamill's *other* definitive role).

A shadowy new figure, the Phantasm, has started picking off figures from Gotham's underworld, with Batman blamed for those sadistic deaths. While the Dark Knight tries to figure out who the Phantasm is and what he might want, Bruce wrestles with the reappearance of his long-lost love Andrea Beaumont (Dana Delaney). Their love story is fleshed out in flashbacks to a time, ten years before, when Bruce was only just beginning his crusade against crime. His relationship with Andrea became so intense that he considered giving up his mission, even awkwardly proposing to her before fate ripped them apart and Bruce, abandoned, took up his mantle once again.

The love story becomes a significant factor in the film, giving us an unusually well-balanced split between Bruce's concerns and those of the Bat. He makes explicit here what most of the films take as read: that being Batman precludes any real relationship and requires a lifelong commitment. Being the Caped Crusader is a sacrifice as well as a vocation that comes with endless cool toys and interesting ways to die. And unusually for a love

interest in one of these things, you can see why Andrea might tempt him away: she's funny, smart and able to knock him flat while he's in the middle of martial-arts practice.

Mark Hamill's Joker, too, is perfectly balanced here between clown and psycho. The Burton and Nolan versions typically default to the latter: understandably, because it's hard to be clownish and yet taken seriously as an adversary in live action. But this is one of the areas where animation offers more flexibility and more room for seemingly contradictory traits: this Joker can flirt with a robot cook and still chill your blood. The Phantasm, too, has

Above Mark Hamill's Joker became his second-most iconic role, only narrowly behind Luke Skywalker.

Opposite For a generation, the Kevin Conroy-voiced Batman is the definitive version.

the sort of cloaked, eerie design that works better in this format than real life, though you may figure out his identity before the revelation finally comes.

This is also an immensely well-stylized film. The visual style is Gotham taken to extremes, with an endlessly vertical city soaring upward in high, Art Deco towers against the dark sky. It's dominated by black and red, often empty of people (too expensive to animate) but always full of menace. Smaller locations are wittily used: when Batman and the Joker brawl in a funland miniature city, it only emphasizes their towering status. The ultra-Gothic score by Shirley Walker also heightens the drama, with those cod-Latin lyrics in the choral opening (actually the names of the music team backwards, claimed Walker), gives the whole a sense of high drama and epic scale.

The plot covers some of the same ground as the Year One and Year Two comics, with Bruce going out in a

Above The Joker wears a jetpack. As he puts it, "Can't be too careful with all those weirdos around."

Opposite Batman battles the mysterious Phantasm – but who could be under the mask?

ski mask on his first mission against criminal thugs and realizing that, while his fight skills might be up to the job, he needs a scarier persona to cow Gotham's underworld. This was designed (at least partly) for a younger audience, so there's a lot of humour. Much of it comes courtesy of Efrem Zimbalist Jr's impeccably groomed Alfred. As Bruce worries about his own state of mind, Alfred reassures him: "What rot, sir. Why, you're the very model of sanity. Oh, by the way, I've pressed your tights and put away your exploding gas balls." Then again, Alfred is also a moral rock, reassuring Bruce that, while he walks "the edge of the abyss", he hasn't fallen in and been consumed by vengeance, as the Phantasm was.

Released with almost no fanfare, *Mask of the Phantasm* flopped at the box office, but it found its fanbase afterward and was followed by a series of WB animated films: notably *Under the Red Hood*, *Batman Beyond: Return of the Joker* and *Batman Ninja*. *Mask of the Phantasm* is not a perfect film – that end-credits ballad by *Wayne's World*'s Tia Carrere couldn't be more 1990s if it wore Doc Martens and a babydoll dress – but it's a deeply satisfying look at what it takes, and what it means, to be Batman.

BLADE
AND BLADE II

THE LATE 1990S WERE A DEEPLY UNCOOL TIME FOR SUPERHEROES. *BATMAN AND ROBIN*, IN 1997, HAD EXTINGUISHED WHAT WAS LEFT OF BATMAN'S CREDIBILITY – AT LEAST TEMPORARILY. JAMES CAMERON'S SPIDER-MAN FILM COULDN'T GET OFF THE GROUND; EVEN HIS OSCAR WOULD NOT TEMPT WARNER BROS TO CAST NICOLAS CAGE AS SUPERMAN.

However, one man single-handedly restored the reputation of the lot and showed that super-films were still a viable concern – because Wesley Snipes signed up to star in *Blade* and changed everything.

Blade wasn't the superhero that Snipes originally wanted to play; he spent years working on a Black Panther movie, getting as far as discussing script ideas with director John Singleton. However, when

that project met a dead end, Snipes looked around and found Blade: in this incarnation a half-human, half-vampire crusader who fights the undead at their own game. It was, Snipes told *The Hollywood Reporter*, "a natural progression and a readjustment"; a more achievable aim. Vampire stories were in the zeitgeist thanks to *Buffy the Vampire Slayer* on TV and the Tom Cruise vehicle *Interview With The Vampire* just

Opposite Blade with Kris Kristofferson's Whistler, who's basically Batman's Alfred with a lot less money and a lot more attitude.

Above Wesley Snipes, with his martial arts training and basso growl, seemed born to play the Daywalker.

a few years before in cinemas. The time was right for a focused, ruthless, leather coat-wearing vigilante to take the bloodsuckers down. To a techno soundtrack.

At that time, Snipes was one of the world's most reliable action stars, and his ferocious martial-arts ability made you believe Blade's one-man crusade could work. He committed to the character too: all grim focus and single-mindedness, careful with his weapons but uninterested in chit-chat. Blade is essentially a blood addict, fighting his own desire for the same food that the vampires crave. In fighting them, he is fighting his own weakness. As his chief ally, Whistler, Kris Kristofferson is the only cast member to come close to Snipes in levels of charisma, though Stephen Dorff, as villain Deacon Frost, deserves credit for somehow carrying off that haircut, and for his excellent taste in shirts.

British director Stephen Norrington, fresh off his cyberpunk debut *Death Machine*, brought it all together – but Snipes was a major force on set, even suggesting Blade's iconic (if slightly baffling) kiss-off line, "Some

motherfucker's always trying to ice-skate uphill." The film was an R-rated hit, grossing over $130 million worldwide on a $45 million budget. Almost none of that money went to the Marvel company itself, but it was proof that even their lesser-known characters had value on the screen. That would be essential as they worked to build their own film empire.

One notion for a sequel was that the first's big bad, La Magra, would turn most of the world's population into vampires for a post-apocalyptic story. That was, perhaps, too constricting or difficult, so instead we get another world-ending threat in the Reapers, a hyper-contagious strain of vampirism that reproduces exponentially. Guillermo del Toro came aboard to direct, in only his second Hollywood film following *Mimic*. He brought with him influences from anime and multiple themes that have punctuated his career: sympathetic monsters, imperilled princesses,

Below Luke Goss went from boy-band heartthrob to Reaper leader in *Blade II*.

grotesquely deformed vampire jaws (see also: *The Strain*), hints of clockwork and gothic architecture. This is by far his goriest movie, however, surpassing the first one in its elements of horror.

The Reapers are led by the mysterious Jared Nomak (Luke "Bros" Goss). To fight them, Blade reluctantly teams with a sort of vampire-SWAT team, the Blood gang, that includes Ron Perlman's Reinhardt and Donnie Yen's underused Snowman. As for his allies, it looked as though N'Bushe Wright's Dr Karen Jenson was being set up to take Whistler's place as Blade's Girl Friday, but by the time the sequel rolled around, she had disappeared from the picture, replaced by Norman Reedus's tech-whizz, Scud. And then, of course, they brought back Whistler, because even in these early days of comic-book movies, the rule of the page carried over: no one stays dead. The

film was another hit, and led directly to del Toro getting the chance to tackle *Hellboy* (see page 48).

The effects haven't all aged well (especially in the sequel) and the attempts to make clubbing in black leather look cool verges on parody, but *Blade* holds up as both a Hollywood game-changer and an action film. *Blade* wasn't the first black superhero: Michael Jai White had beaten Snipes to the punch in *Spawn*, and there had been earlier comedic films, such as *Meteor Man*, *Blankman* and, in 1977, *Abar: The First Black Superman*. But *Blade* was the one that went bigger, which convinced Hollywood that superhero films could work for adults as well as family audiences, and that you didn't need Batman or Superman levels of name recognition to translate a comic star to the screen. If the idea was sufficiently good, it would sell worldwide anyway. And that made all the difference.

BLADE: TRINITY

If the first two films had almost parodic levels of cool, the third had almost none. Screenwriter David S. Goyer stepped up to direct, but new, younger characters in Jessica Biel's Abigail Whistler and Ryan Reynolds' Hannibal King couldn't make up for Snipes's waning interest and leaden action set-pieces. Worse, Dominic Purcell was badly miscast as

Dracula/Drake, the uber-threat who's not that bad, and draws focus from Parker Posey's much more fun Danica. At least Reynolds shows some aptitude for wisecracking comic-book characters with swords who enjoy creative swearing, with a standout line involving jugging, and thunder and otherwise too rude to print.

X-MEN AND
X2: X-MEN UNITED

AUSCHWITZ AND A WEARY PARADE OF PRISONERS ARE SORTED BY SADISTIC NAZI

GUARDS. A TEENAGE BOY IS RIPPED AWAY FROM HIS ELDERLY PARENTS, AND FIGHTS

TO GET BACK TO THEM, REACHING OUT DESPERATELY.

But they're led away through the gates toward a looming building, chimney reaching skyward, and the struggling boy is pulled in the other direction by the armed guards, and the guard dogs bark frantically, and then somehow the gates start to creak and *bend* toward the struggling boy, opening further and further.

It's a bold opening for a superhero movie, supposedly a popcorn genre, and it was certainly controversial. Then again, the X-Men always had a thick streak of social commentary. Created in the 1960s at the height of the US Civil Rights movement, its heroes were part of a feared minority – super-powered mutants who live among humanity but are not accepted by them. Such themes became more pointed and obvious over time, especially in those stories involving Magneto (Ian McKellen's metal-controlling character), a Holocaust survivor who becomes a militant fighter for mutant freedom. The philosophical difference between his revolutionary goals and Patrick Stewart's telepathic Professor Charles Xavier, whose mutant students protect humanity in the hope of winning the hearts and minds of the majority, was a deliberate echo of the Malcolm X/Martin Luther King tactical divide.

The *X-Men* comics are big sellers, but comics readers are a relatively small audience; it was the 1990s cartoon series that made it clear this gang could appeal to the wider world. The live-action film, therefore, amped up the realism and parallels to our own world

Above Patrick Stewart's Professor X and Ian McKellen's Magneto face off across the chessboard.

Opposite The franchise's breakout star, Hugh Jackman as Wolverine.

(particularly in the second film's "Have you tried not being a mutant?" coming-out scene) to give it heft. As, of course, did casting people like Stewart and McKellen.

The single most important decision, however, concerned the quick-healing, metal-boned, partially amnesiac Wolverine. The perennially popular character is our way in to the X-Men, and Hugh Jackman, who played him, became the film's breakout star. Jackman's casting was a happy accident: he was plucked from playing *Oklahoma!* onstage at London's National Theatre after the *Mission: Impossible 2* shoot ran long and original choice, Dougray Scott, was conflicted out. With everything to prove, Jackman the song-and-dance man trained like a demon and

took cold showers (the better to act short-tempered) every day for months to get into character as the X-Men's grumpy mascot. That nascent star power, balanced by the two elder statesmen, set the tone: this franchise would deal with big questions while a quippy brawler with claws in his hands took bad guys apart. In a technique that would be repeated throughout the series (and one drawn straight from the comics) he was paired – non-romantically! – with a teenage girl, traumatized power-vampire Rogue (Anna Paquin), and their wary relationship gave the film a heart beneath all the politicking and punching.

The sequel upgrades the action and ups the stakes. It opens with a frenetic, thrilling attack on the White House by Alan Cumming's teleporting Nightcrawler, and manages to more or less maintain that level. There's Wolverine going berserk and taking down a SWAT team. There's the giant Colossus in his "organic steel" armoured form. There's Magneto's impossibly cool escape from prison and Lady Deathstrike's battle, with that ruthless end move. It's not all about huge effects, but it's full of fan-pleasing, plot-relevant moments that work.

Opposite Brian Cox, as bad guy Stryker, sets out to destroy all mutants.

Below Halle Berry's Storm and Alan Cumming's Nightcrawler prepare for a rescue mission.

X-MEN: THE LAST STAND

A mutant cure causes division between those who welcome their powers and those who just want to be normal, but a bigger problem has emerged from beneath the waters of Alkali Lake. Jean Grey (Famke Janssen) has emerged as the unstoppable Phoenix. The Phoenix storyline was a highlight of the animated series. Alas, the film version fumbles it amid a mess of new characters and poor casting choices (Vinnie Jones as Juggernaut, Ben Foster as Angel) that detract from Jean's story. There are still great moments and impressive effects (the de-ageing of Stewart and McKellen was groundbreaking) but it's a lesser entry in the X-canon.

Admittedly, all the moving parts mean that we don't get to spend time with everyone. Rogue suffers a big fall-off in screen time but Halle Berry's Storm is, as usual, probably the worst short-changed, though her brief scenes with Nightcrawler show why she deserved more. But everyone gets at least a moment to show who they are, and new bad guy William Stryker (Brian Cox) makes a formidable adversary.

The stage was set for an epic trilogy, until *Superman Returns* lured the original director away and Brett Ratner's *X-Men: The Last Stand* fumbled the last act. Still, these two X-films built on the momentum that

Blade had established and hinted at what superhero movies could become: character-driven stories touching on real issues. *X-Men* was the first producing credit for Kevin Feige, who would become head of Marvel Studios and launch the intricately interlaced Marvel Cinematic Universe (see page 66). This was also the first modern superhero film to give us a final shot – a blurry, Phoenix-shaped light under the surface of a lake – to tease superfans in the audience into a frenzy. Suddenly, we saw that superhero movies could tell huge stories – the sort of thing that only animation had previously dared. The world was opening up.

SPIDER-MAN
AND SPIDER-MAN 2

SOME SUPERHEROES ARE GODLIKE CHARACTERS WHOSE POWERS ENABLE THEM TO NEGOTIATE THE WORLD ON A DIFFERENT LEVEL TO OUR OWN. THEN THERE'S SPIDER-MAN, A KID GRANTED EXTRAORDINARY POWER BUT NOT – AND THIS IS CRUCIAL – THE ABILITY TO GET TO CLASS ON TIME. JACK KIRBY AND STAN LEE'S BIG-HEARTED WEBSLINGER WAS THE FIRST MAJOR COMIC-BOOK SUPERHERO WHOSE LIFE WAS MADE VISIBLY HARDER BY HIS TRANSFORMATION.

This was no billionaire with all the material comforts in the world to ease his path; no inhuman creature with a separate world to draw upon. Peter Parker is a smart and somewhat nerdy kid, in a family struggling to make ends meet. But he was given great power, and with great power comes... oh, you know.

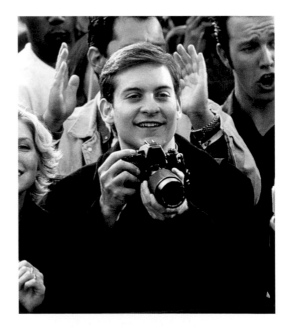

Sam Raimi's *Spider-Man* films were a monster success but have been overshadowed by later efforts, so it's worth remembering their impact. Visual effects had just reached the point where they could bring Spidey fully to life, swinging along the New York streets and whooping as he went. The sense of sheer joy and freedom as Tobey Maguire's Peter explores his spidey-powers is infectious; in an immediately post-9/11 world, there was something transporting about seeing New York bathed in a magic-hour glow, transformed into a playground for a skinny kid suddenly imbued with spider-powers. Raimi's films reflect Spider-Man's basic optimism even in their darkest moments. It's what the world needed in the summer of 2002.

Some bits have stood up less well. Maguire is, by some distance, the wettest Spider-Man, almost a parody of a gee-whizz good-hearted kid, rather than

the thing itself. But then he's abetted by the wettest love interest in Kirsten Dunst's Mary Jane (literally soaked, during their iconic rain-sodden kiss) and easily the most saccharine Aunt May from Rosemary Harris.

While there was controversy at the time about his immobile helmet mask, Willem Dafoe's Green

Goblin has aged better. His descent into psychosis set the tone for any number of bad-guy origin stories, but few that followed can channel the same grinning malice as Dafoe – especially in that brutal final fight. Earlier, his Goblin scream of, "We'll meet again, Spider-Man!" as he bugs out is a classic Marvel-comics moment. Though, while Dafoe is good, by far the best casting is J. K. Simmons' J. Jonah Jameson, the meanest (in more than one sense) newspaper editor in film history. He deserved the Oscar for this, long before *Whiplash*.

Above, Opposite Tobey Maguire's *Spider-Man* was the box-office hit who proved what superhero movies could do and opened the way for the floor that followed.

On release, the biggest controversy involved Spidey's organic web-shooters, an ability that came with his spider-powers instead of from mechanical slingers. Really, it just speeds up the storytelling (though if the spider silk is organic, shouldn't it be emerging, ahem, lower down?) and isn't the most offensive thing here. It's the gooey relationship stuff and the broad comedy – much of it drawn straight from the comics that Raimi adored in his youth – that now feels out of place. The effects occasionally look video-game, but they've aged much better than the casual homophobia (Spidey's trashtalk includes "That's a cool outfit; did your husband give it to you?")

Still, there's loads to love. The supporting cast features a pre-fame Octavia Spencer, and Elizabeth Banks, Bill Nunn, Aasif Mandvi, Randy Savage

and, of course, Raimi's good-luck charm in Bruce
Campbell. Raimi's more idiosyncratic touches work
beautifully, with the Goblin's fights just a little sped up
and a board-room scene that unabashedly quotes *The
Hudsucker Proxy* (Raimi collaborated with the Coen
Brothers on that script). This was a phenomenon,
the first film to make over $100 million in its opening
weekend (beating the first *Harry Potter*), and it
still looks pretty good if you avoid comparing it to
Homecoming or *Into The Spider-Verse* (see pages 152
and 180).

Spider-Man 2 is even better, mostly thanks to
Alfred Molina's Doctor Octopus ("Guy named Otto
Octavius winds up with eight limbs... what are the
odds?" Jameson crows). Perhaps surprisingly, Doc
Ock is one of the most nuanced of Spidey's rogues'
gallery – collectively, the best gang of ne'er-do-wells
in the Marvel Universe – and even swapped minds

SPIDER-MAN 3

Super-trilogies too often fall into a
predictable pattern: origin story, hero
quits, hero goes bad. Spider-Man
follows the trend into a symbiote-
suit flirtation with selfishness, but
that's not the biggest problem here.
It's the surfeit of bad guys. There's
the lingering matter of Harry
Osborne's Green Goblin II, the tragic
Sandman (Thomas Haden Church)
and, eventually, the symbiote Venom
(Topher Grace), who bonds with
Eddie Brock after Peter rejects it.
It's overstuffed and overlong, and
there's a sense that Raimi's heart
isn't in Venom in particular. Better
to have set up the symbiote this time
and left the battle against Venom
for a fourth film, instead of one
messy blow-out party that wiped out
the franchise.

with Peter Parker once, whereupon he chose to act the hero, just as Peter had. Here, he's mad with grief and the pain of having his cybernetic arms accidentally fused to his body, their own malignant AI overriding his higher instincts, and Molina turns on a dime from sneering supervillain to bereaved victim. His operating-room emergence as Doc Ock, shot by Raimi in a hyper-kinetic style that recalls his *Evil Dead* breakthrough, is perfect.

Opposite Spidey's iconic upside-down kiss with Mary-Jane (Kirsten Dunst).

Below James Franco as Harry Osborne, the second Goblin.

Overleaf Spidey faced off with Alfred Molina's Doc Ock in what remains one of the great superhero movie showdowns.

Meanwhile, Peter finds his power deserting him as he starts to doubt himself, and finally quits the Spider-game – only to swing back into action when Doc Ock begins his reign of terror. Once again, the weak link is the schmaltzy love scenes (MJ's claim that "I have always been standing in your doorway" is just awful, and also untrue), which is a shame in contrast to the short but sweet love story between Otto and Rosalie (Donna Murphy).

But those first two films were a breath of fresh air; a reminder that superhero movies can work for kids as well as adults – even if the violence sometimes dances on the edge of respectability. If *Blade* and the *X-Men* showed Hollywood that you didn't need Superman-levels of name recognition to make a big-screen superhero movie, *Spider-Man* reminded them that familiarity really helps.

THE GREATEST
MOVIE SUPERVILLAINS

THEY'RE THE BAD GUYS SO DASTARDLY THAT WE CAN'T HELP BUT LOVE THEM REALLY.

LOKI

PLAYED BY: TOM HIDDLESTON
FILMS: THOR TRILOGY, AVENGERS

The dangerously charming Loki has swayed a little inconsistently over four movies between "loveable rogue" and "murderous scumbag" – but somehow, he's strangely irresistible either way.

THE JOKER

PLAYED BY: HEATH LEDGER
FILM: THE DARK KNIGHT

The only superhero performance ever to win an Oscar, Ledger's Joker is unforgettable. From his pencil-trick introduction to his cackling, lip-smacking grin.

BULLSEYE

PLAYED BY: COLIN FARRELL
FILM: DAREDEVIL

A bright spot in an otherwise slightly colourless effort, Farrell's egotistical bad guy with the deadly aim doesn't take himself nearly as seriously as the rest of the movie. Except when he misses.

DOC OCK

PLAYED BY: ALFRED MOLINA
FILM: SPIDER-MAN 2

"The power of my sun... in the palm of my hand!" There's a hint of mono-mania to Otto Octavius even before the tragedy that makes him Doc Ock, but his ability to mix implacable enmity and relatable humanity makes him memorable.

THANOS

PLAYED BY: JOSH BROLIN
FILM: AVENGERS: INFINITY WAR & ENDGAME

No purple dude with a wrinkly chin should be scary enough to challenge half the Avengers, let alone all of them plus friends. Except Thanos, the warlord who raged across planets before destroying half the universe in a blink; he gave them a run for their money.

HELA

PLAYED BY: CATE BLANCHETT
FILM: THOR: RAGNAROK

It's good, sometimes, to see a two-time Oscar winner just cut loose. And Cate Blanchett clearly has a blast as the Norse death goddess, who takes only minutes to conquer Asgard and, as a bonus, rides a giant zombie wolf.

CATWOMAN

PLAYED BY: MICHELLE PFEIFFER
FILM: BATMAN RETURNS

Slinky, sexy and unpredictable as hell, Michelle Pfeiffer's Catwoman isn't a full-blown villain, perhaps – more of an antagonist. But she blows up a department store for kicks so she's not exactly a good girl either.

GENERAL ZOD

PLAYED BY: TERENCE STAMP
FILM: SUPERMAN II

It takes a lot to challenge Superman, but the ruthless Kryptonian war leader will do the job. Michael Shannon's version is remarkably effective, but Stamp's original is still the definitive portrayal. You have to admire a man who can conquer the world in a puffy shirt..

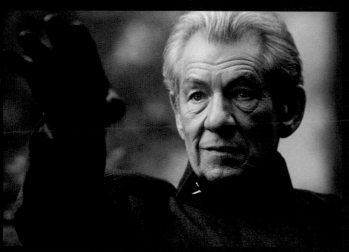

MAGNETO

PLAYED BY: IAN MCKELLEN
FILM: X-MEN SERIES

"We are the future, Charles. Not them. They no longer matter." Magneto sets out his mutant-rights stall early in the X-franchise, but his intelligence makes him unpredictable. He can sometimes be talked into doing the right thing – but he might yet betray his allies.

BARON ZEMO

PLAYED BY: DANIEL BRUHL
FILM: CAPTAIN AMERICA: CIVIL WAR

This character provoked mixed reactions, but in terms of bringing their plans to fruition, Zemo got further than almost anyone else on the list (Thanos, maybe), and did it all with a near-surgical application of force.

MYSTIQUE

PLAYED BY: REBECCA ROMIJN
FILMS: X-MEN SERIES

Later ret-conned, badly, into a good guy, Mystique was really born to be bad. Romijn's shapeshifter is a true believer in Magneto's cause, a remarkably effective agent and a ferocious fighter. And she does it all basically naked. Now that's formidable.

ERIK KILLMONGER

PLAYED BY: MICHAEL B. JORDAN
FILM: BLACK PANTHER

Ruthless, bloodthirsty and very nearly unstoppable, Killmonger combines the worst elements of a berserker with the thinking of a master strategist. He's also an absolutely terrifying physical opponent, as his scars – one for every kill – demonstrate neatly.

HULK

WHEN DIRECTOR ANG LEE FIRST MET WITH DENNIS MUREN AND HIS EFFECTS TEAM FOR HULK, HE PRESENTED THEM WITH HIS REFERENCE MATERIAL FOR THE MONSTER. INSTEAD OF THE USUAL STORYBOARDS OR COMIC-BOOK PANELS, THERE WAS A DRY PIECE OF DESERT WOOD, A SMALL SANDBOX AND A ROCK WITH SOME RED LICHEN ON ONE SIDE. OBVIOUSLY.

Perhaps that's what one should expect when an Oscar-nominated auteur takes on a superhero film. Lee had just been accaimed for the wuxia masterpiece *Crouching Tiger, Hidden Dragon*, and would win Best Director for his next film, *Brokeback Mountain*. But right in the middle there is this big angry green guy – something that Lee approached as enthusiastically as any of his more "respectable" outings – and a film in which he says he had more freedom and support than he had ever enjoyed before.

Initially, the marriage works pretty well. Lee experiments with the philosophical side of the Hulk, delving into not just the physical damage that made him but also the emotional trauma that underpins it.

Opposite Director Ang Lee pushed hard to make Hulk the most believable CG-character yet.

Below Eric Bana as tormented scientist Bruce Banner.

This Hulk's first, nighttime appearance is straight out of Frankenstein, hulking out of the shadows, but he has weirdly thoughtful moments too, taking a moment to admire a desert scene while on the run. This is a monster composed of different shades of, er, green. In this telling, Eric Bana's Bruce Banner is hit with gamma radiation again and again, surviving each blast because of something in his blood. That something was inherited from the self-experiments of his mad-scientist father, David Banner (Nick Nolte, playing a comics character renamed in tribute to the TV show).

The science only partially explains Bruce's power; the rage he has known ever since David killed his mother is the other key. There are repeated references to "something inside" the reined-in Bruce. His lab partner and ex-girlfriend, Betty Ross (Jennifer Connelly), complains that he's not sufficiently passionate, but better to say it's a passion too deeply hidden. "Bruce Banner's dream is Hulk's reality," said Lee. As Bruce begins to grapple with the buried memories that David's reappearance uncovers, the Hulk wakes up and shakes off the shackles that Bruce placed upon his rage.

For a film that sometimes verges on Steve Ditko-style surrealism with its microscopic imagery (taken from work by Lee's scientist wife, Jane Lin) and memories dissolving into desert sand, Lee draws from more traditional comics as well. There is humour in the steadily mounting injuries of Josh Lucas's Talbot or in the way that Sam Elliott's General Ross spits "mutant French poodle". He uses inset panels, split-screens and layered frames to recreate the feeling of your eye flicking from panel to panel. The Hulk is a lurid, print-inspired shade of emerald – a glaring colour compared to the more olive-toned monster that would follow in *Avengers*. But the effects are otherwise impressive for the era: watch the ripples as bullets hit Hulk's skin or the shift of muscles underneath.

There are still frustrations, however. It's too neat that David and Ross, Betty's father, worked together years before. And it goes wildly off the rails at the end. After a too-short rampage through San Francisco, Hulk allows himself to be tamed by Betty like a precious unicorn accepting a virgin's bridle. He melts back into Bruce and is taken into custody, where he's subjected to Nick Nolte. "I gave you life; now you must give it back to me," Nolte's

Above Nick Nolte's David Banner confronts his son.

David rants. "Stop your bawling, you weak little speck of human trash." He turns into a weird cross between the comic-book villains Absorbing Man and Zzzax, setting the scene for a baffling final fight through the clouds and into a lake that General Ross gamma-bombs in a final *coup de grace*.

It's an ending that makes more metaphorical sense than narrative: after demanding that Bruce surrender his rage, David Banner is overwhelmed by it. He can't endure the anger that animates Hulk, so that he is – apparently – dying even before both are bombed. The message here is that only Bruce has what it takes to become the Hulk.

They survive the hit and escape south in the form of Banner acting as an itinerant aid worker in the jungles. The wandering do-gooder model reflects the old TV show and would more or less survive into the Marvel Cinematic Universe (MCU – see page 66) – about the only idea here that does.

Universal Studios and Marvel were, ultimately, right to take a swing on Lee – that style-switching savant who brings something new to every genre he touches. This is a deeply strange film, mixing bombast and beauty, philosophy and throw-downs, but Lee's oddball Hulk is far more satisfying than the more obvious brawler that would follow.

THE INCREDIBLE HULK

Louis LeTerrier's MCU film not only recasts its leads but ret-cons its predecessor in the opening credits. Edward Norton makes a credible Bruce Banner, and William Hurt is almost as good as Elliott despite the lesser growl, but this one is a more conventional super-film. If only bad guy the Abomination, aka Tim Roth's Emil Blonsky, weren't a horrendous mess of a design and the Hulk didn't have that Bon Jovi hair as he howls at the storm. On the up side, the Hulk's "boxing gloves" are great and it led to one of the funnier lines in *Avengers*, when Bruce sheepishly admits that "Last time I was in New York I broke... Harlem." So careless.

HELLBOY AND
HELLBOY II: THE GOLDEN ARMY

FOR AGES, OSCAR-WINNING DIRECTOR GUILLERMO DEL TORO HAD HOLLYWOOD

FOOLED. EVERYONE THOUGHT HE HAD A ONE-FOR-THEM, ONE-FOR-ME MODEL;

THAT HE WOULD MAKE A COMMERCIAL FILM LIKE *HELLBOY* OR *PACIFIC RIM* AND

THEN CRAFT A SMALLER, MORE PERSONAL PROJECT LIKE *PAN'S LABYRINTH* OR

THE SHAPE OF WATER.

But what proponents of this theory failed to grasp is how much del Toro adores monsters. His vampires, demons and kaiju are as close to his heart as any arthouse hero could ever be, and almost certainly closer than his Oscars. And perhaps none of his mainstream leads were so made for him as Mike Mignola's likeable, misunderstood Hellboy.

The comic was a cult success rather than a massive mainstream hit, but it had a cool title and an instantly recognizable hero, and its blend of comedy, horror and adventure seemed tailor-made for the superhero milieu of the early 2000s. That meant something with personality and a point of view, but capable of working on a relatively restrained budget. And it was a cool premise: our hero is a being conjured from hell by a Nazi sorcerer and destined to restore the Lovecraftian elder gods. Alas for the fascists and nihilists, Hellboy grows up with a taste for fighting the forces of evil, smoking cigars and keeping pet kittens.

The key decision Del Toro made was hiring Ron Perlman to play his lead. This was a man well used to prosthetics, thanks to TV's *Beauty and the Beast*, *The Island Of Doctor Moreau* and del Toro's own *Blade II*. More to the point, Perlman out of make-up seemed like a Hellboy kind of guy: down to Earth and blunt-speaking, fond of the finer things but no metrosexual, politically liberal and feminist. He's the ideal mix of tough and touchy-feely.

Almost as important was Hellboy's team, led by Doug Jones' heroic amphibian Abe Sapien (voiced in the first film by David Hyde Pierce) and Selma Blair's firestarter Liz. They provide, respectively, the more intellectual and more cautious counterparts to Hellboy's bombastic style. They also comprise his family, alongside the late John Hurt's Professor Bruttenholm, the researcher who raised him from a hellbaby. It's this group's sense of closeness and affection that sets this apart from other monster movies and many superhero efforts. 'Big Red' is a gruff, bad-tempered and impatient fool at times, but these (more reliable) guys love him – and so we follow their lead.

In its world building, *Hellboy* is something of a cross between *X-Men* and *Men In Black*, with just a dash of *Constantine*. Monsters and fairies exist, and it's the job of the Bureau Of Paranormal Research And Development to keep them out from under our bed. That's particularly true of Nazi necromancer Kroenen (Ladislav Beran) in the first film and the second film's big bad, the significantly more sympathetic elf-rights activist Prince Nuada (Luke Goss).

Opposite Ron Perlman and Guillermo del Toro had been collaborating for years before *Hellboy*, most notably in 1993's excellent vampire flick, *Cronos*.

Neither film is perfect. Both plots sometimes feel like a distraction from the character piece we'd rather be watching, the one where Hellboy and his mates simply ride around in a garbage truck to tilt at monsters, and the pacing can verge on TV show languor. Nuada's story in the second film is almost a replay of the plot of *Blade II*: a prince threatens humanity and his father's status quo; his sister is sympathetic to our heroes; Ron Perlman is involved.

Still, despite budget limitations and occasionally ropey early-2000s CG, *Hellboy* remains oddly charming. His prosthetics, and Perlman's ability to emote through them, are superb. Nor is he alone in that: Abe Sapien would give these films enough heart to sustain them singlehanded, with his fussy mannerisms and extreme bravery. Del Toro even makes you root for the love story between the shy, traumatized Liz and his hulking hero; no mean feat when the guy has devil horns and a fist made out of

rock, and she risks burning down entire city blocks if she loses control.

Like Mignola's comics, the *Hellboy* films were destined to be cult favourites rather than box-office behemoths, but they have endured surprisingly well. Put that down to del Toro's genuine empathy for monsters – look at Hellboy's reluctant, heartbreaking fight against a unique Elemental in the second film – and a cast who gave us reason to root for them. The combination was always guaranteed to make us feel sympathy for the devil.

Top Big fist, big gun. There's a theme here...

Opposite, left Ladislav Beran as Kroenen, showing off some typically brilliant costume design.

Opposite, right Luke Goss once again took on a supernatural villain role for del Toro.

HELLBOY (2019)

Neil Marshall's reboot of the franchise is a significantly bloodier and more violent affair than del Toro's work. David Harbour does good work as the horned hero, and he gets a whole slew of daddy issues to wrestle into submission alongside his various giants, changelings and witches. But there's little sense of a Scooby gang around him. Sasha Lane's medium, Alice, is too busy struggling with her accent to focus and Daniel Dae-Kim's paramilitary Ben Daimo is too secretive to make much connection. This might yet start a new era for Hellboy, thanks to its end-credit teasers, but as a standalone film it needed another few drafts of the script.

CONSTANTINE

JOHN CONSTANTINE IS A BLOND LIVERPUDLIAN WHO EXORCISES DEMONS WHEN HE'S NOT CHAIN-SMOKING. AT LEAST, HE IS IN THE COMICS. SO THERE WAS GENERAL CONSTERNATION WHEN THE BIG-SCREEN VERSION CAST KEANU REEVES AND MOVED THE STORY TO LA.

Wrong hair colour, wrong city, wrong guy – right? Even his trench coat had gone from tan to black. But if history shows us anything, it's that you should never bet against Keanu. Move past that basic heresy and you'll find a seriously underrated slice of supernatural comic-book fun, one that's every bit as inventive as *Hellboy* but – with respect to Mike Mignola's creation – a lot more handsome. And it retains far more of the *Hellblazer* comics' attitude than its critics were willing to acknowledge.

This Constantine has been tortured by the ability to see demons, ghosts and monsters since he was a child, to the extent that he attempted suicide as a teenager, rather than have to endure the horrors that were driving him mad. His attempt means that he's destined for hell, whenever the time comes, and yet he spends his days exorcizing the demons that will one day be charged with tormenting him, perhaps hoping to earn his way back into Heaven's good books. Yet as the half-angel Gabriel (Tilda Swinton) tells him, that very motivation means that none of his good deeds can count for much.

The remove to LA is actually a pretty good fit for Constantine, who is a sort of occult PI, after all. This is, therefore, less the beachside Los Angeles and azure skies of, say, *Baywatch* – the sun appears perhaps twice in this entire film – and more the LA noir familiar from crime thrillers of the 1940s. This

Above John Constantine (Keanu Reeves) weaponises his tattoos against the forces of darkness.

Opposite Constantine ventures into an arid, desolate Hell-version of LA in search of answers.

isn't literally in black and white and shades of grey, except morally, but it feels awfully close.

The flashpoint is the suicide of Izzy (Rachel Weisz). Her sister, Angela (also Weisz), is convinced that the suicide was staged, despite Isabelle's long history of mental illness, and enlists Constantine to investigate. In the course of the investigation, he learns that something strange is going on in Hell and on Earth: full-blooded demons, who are supposedly banished from the mortal plane, are breaking through, and half-demons are searching for the fabled Spear of Destiny, which has just been uncovered. Cue lots of growled explanations to the clueless Angela and a tour through LA's supernatural community as Constantine tries to find out what's going on. Oh, and he's fighting terminal lung cancer in a storyline drawn from Garth Ennis's *Dangerous Habits* comic-book arc.

It's a fun sort of mystery: less a whodunnit and more a what's-being-done. But director Francis Lawrence bathes the film in style. The portrayals of Hell are William Blake by way of the nuclear war dreams in *Terminator 2*, and his crowds of half-angels, half-demons and shamans are *just* close enough to LA hipsters that they could make you look askance at any merely cool people you see in the days after watching. After, Djimon Hounsou's Midnite

Above A bedraggled Rachel Weisz as Angela .

Opposite, top Constantine, witch doctor Papa Midnite (Djimon Hounsou) and John's sidekick Chas (Shia LaBeouf).

Opposite, bottom Demons gotta demon.

looks like any exceptionally handsome person you might see in a club, and Gavin Rossdale's half-demon Balthazar seems like just another yuppie.

Reeves is also really good, his laconic delivery reading here as bad attitude rather than laid-back surfer dude. His Constantine is utterly pissed off with basically everyone; he can be magnificently condescending and devil-may-care (no pun intended), even with the people he likes. But he's also highly competent as both a detective and a mystic, judiciously using his connections and abilities to investigate our world and the Other Side, and arming himself heavily enough to see off most threats. But when it comes down to it, it's trickery, cunning and a willingness to go further than his opponents expect that wins the day, and it's cheering to watch a guy who wins the day mainly on brain-power – and against Peter Stormare's Lucifer, no less.

It's not a flawless film; the less said about Shia LaBeouf's teenage sidekick and his attempts at comic relief, the better. But it's far better than you've heard, and one of the most effectively stylized and visually inventive comic-book movies out there. Perhaps we shouldn't term Constantine a "superhero"; he certainly isn't in the capes-and-tights sense. But he can do what others cannot, go where others fear to tread, and take down whatever evil he finds there. Constantine may rely more on tricks, know-how and clever weaponry to take down the opposition, but then again, so does Batman. The important thing is that he sees evil wiles and then smites them – and gives the devil the finger while he's about it.

THE DARK KNIGHT TRILOGY

BATMAN AND ROBIN DIDN'T JUST KILL THE BATMAN FRANCHISE – IT CUT IT UP INTO TINY PIECES, CREMATED THOSE, SCATTERED THE ASHES TO THE WIND AND SALTED THE EARTH WHERE ONCE SEQUELS GREW. IT WOULD TAKE A MIRACLE TO RESURRECT THE DARK KNIGHT AS A SERIOUS CINEMA PROSPECT. OR, AS IT TURNED OUT, IT WOULD TAKE AN ENGLISHMAN WITH A PLAN TO TAKE BATMAN BACK TO THE START AND REBUILD HIM FROM THE GROUND UP.

In 2002, director Christopher Nolan was coming from his inventively told *Memento* and the Al Pacino-starring thriller *Insomnia*. He had a good reputation as a creative, unconventional filmmaker and looked ready for the step to big-budget studio work. More importantly, he had a vision for Batman – and after the excess of the Joel Schumacher films, perhaps it was the only way to go. He would explain why a man chooses to dress like a rodent to fight crime. He would take the story back to first principles, the boy and his butler who create a vigilante, and give Batman back his pride. He cast Christian Bale in the lead – a serious and talented actor who hadn't quite hit the A-list at that point – and the likeable Katie Holmes opposite him as his childhood friend turned crusading lawyer, Rachel Dawes. Then Nolan surrounded both with mature, recognizable faces:

Opposite Bale's Batman was the first incarnation of the character able to turn his head in the Bat-cowl.

Below Bruce Wayne (Christian Bale) and Alfred (Michael Caine) prepare to party.

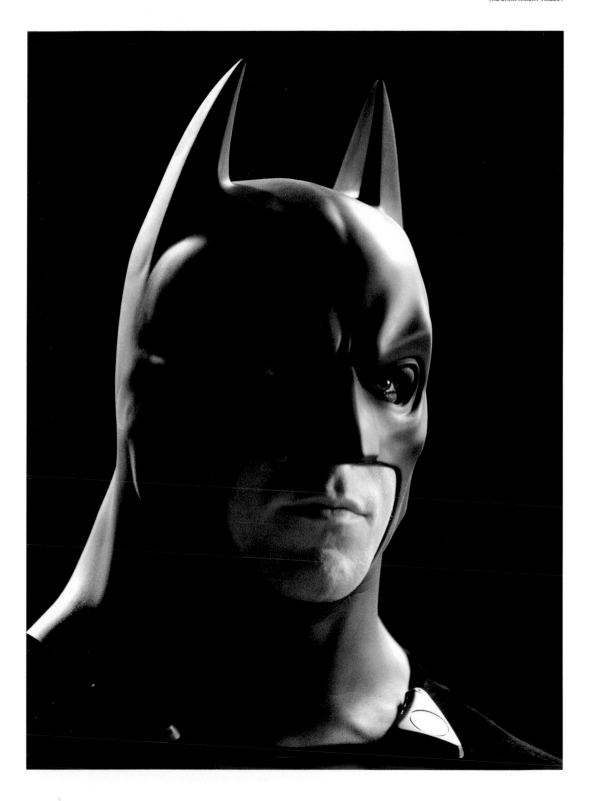

Michael Caine as loyal retainer, Alfred; Liam Neeson as Bruce's mentor, "Henri Ducard"; Morgan Freeman as impish tech genius, Lucius Fox; and Gary Oldman as Gotham's one honest cop, Lieutenant Jim Gordon.

That first film, *Batman Begins*, roots itself in something like reality, a world in which crime bosses play the system to avoid jail and cops take bribes or risk the suspicion of their fellows. But this is still *Batman*, so it can't be too grounded, so the Mob's friendly psychiatrist, Dr Jonathan Crane, is also a psycho called the Scarecrow who weaponizes fear itself. Bruce Wayne travels the world in his youth, studying crime and criminals, learning martial arts and training himself for a mission that has not fully taken shape in his head. That's all fine. But the secretive "League of Shadows", training somewhere high in the Himalayas to take down cities and manipulate civilization itself, is more of a leap.

Nolan and his fellow screenwriter, David S. Goyer, drew from many of the comics – Commissioner Jim Gordon (Gary Oldman) owes a lot to *Year One*; Nolan found short story "The Man Who Falls" helpful as a way into Bruce himself – but this is not even a loose adaptation of any one title. The tone is darker and more restrained than any previous Batman film, even the well-regarded animated ones (see page 22), and there was no single, stand-out action moment in the trailer that would sell it as a must-see to audiences who were not familiar with the whole "reboot" concept (oh, those innocent days!) and didn't see why they should care. Perhaps as a result of that reserve, it was not an immediate box-office sensation, taking a respectable but hardly stellar $374m worldwide. Blame the lingering stench of *Batman and Robin*, however, because its reputation only grew and its home entertainment performance was markedly more solid, allowing a sequel, *The Dark Knight*, to be greenlit. And that would change everything.

By this time, the fans were onboard, but their attention came with strings. The casting of Heath Ledger as the Joker was met with consternation and even outrage. How could this teen heartthrob, as most of them knew him, possibly match up to Jack Nicholson? Then came the first images in *Empire* magazine – Ledger in a cell with that streaked make-

up and Glasgow grin – and people started to trust. As it turned out, his performance would electrify the film, making the Joker an entirely unpredictable force of chaos with a twisted sense of humour. Who else would dress his hostages up as kidnappers? Who else would introduce himself with a "magic trick" like that? And how else to explain his aim to bring out the madness in everyone?

The Joker, done well, has always been Batman's dark mirror. Batman exercises absolute self-control and self-discipline to serve order; the Joker acts exactly as he will in order to promote chaos. Both act outside the law; both plan far more meticulously than they would admit (though the Joker's plan, written down, makes less than no sense) and both become obsessed with the other. "Criminals aren't complicated, Alfred," Bruce claims at one point; the Joker will show him otherwise, and push him to find his own limits. It's a magnificent face-off, "What happens when an unstoppable force meets an immovable object," as the Joker calls it.

Opposite Batman's mission to an asylum ends with a daring escape, including this leap down a quickly bat-infested staircase.

Top Morgan Freeman plays newly created character Lucius Fox, a sort of corporate Q to Batman's Bond.

Above Maggie Gyllenhaal took over the role of Rachel Dawes from Katie Holmes after the first film.

Opposite Heath Ledger's chaotic, unpredictable Joker was a barnstorming, never-matched superhero movie performance.

After both the success of *The Dark Knight* and the tragedy of Heath Ledger's early death, however, the third part of the trilogy was still to come. Nolan faced the not inconsiderable challenge of finding another bad guy who could step into this world. The solution, in *The Dark Knight Rises*, was Tom Hardy's Bane, the hulking mercenary who could overwhelm Batman physically but also match him in plotting and investigation (remember the gasp when audiences realized what vault Bane was attempting to break into?). He frames his – successful! – takeover of Gotham as a sort of populist revolution, turning poor against rich and threatening the entire city with destruction if he doesn't get his way. It's a logical progression from the Joker's schemes against hospitals and ferries, or even the first film's takeover of the "Narrows" district.

There's a lot going on in *The Dark Knight Rises*, with Bruce overcoming injury, being beaten and imprisoned and having to build himself back up, and then facing that final threat. There are (perhaps too many) new characters, including Marion Cotillard's Miranda Tate/Talia Al'Ghul, Joseph Gordon Levitt's John Robin Blake and Anne Hathaway's Catwoman. By this point, Nolan commanded an absurdly deep bench of talent: Burn Gorman and Aiden Gillen get a single scene each; Glen Powell gets a couple of lines as a stock trader. Most distracting is the film's odd anti-populist stance: though it was filmed at the time of the Occupy movement, it explicitly aligns its bad guys with the 99 per cent and has a billionaire saving the day. It plays better several years on than it did at the time.

Nolan's a smart filmmaker, though not always a subtle one. If you play a drinking game every time someone mentions "fear" or a synonym thereof in the first film, you'll be endangering your liver's health; same with ideas of order and chaos in the sequel, or questions of "resilience" and "rising" from defeat in the third. There are questions in these films that remain controversial among Bat-fans: it's hard to deny that he kills people or recklessly risks doing so in every film, arguably breaking Batman's "one rule" (though the comics have done as much). Worse, between *The Dark Knight* and *The Dark Knight Rises*, he is said to have retired from action for years at a time, an anathema to the Caped Crusader's lifelong devotion to his mission.

And yet these quibbles have not prevented this trilogy from becoming the definitive Batman arc for a generation of fans. Nolan's films showed that superhero movies could offer serious drama, with *The Dark Knight* becoming the first of its breed to gain serious traction in a Best Picture campaign at the Academy Awards (the film was not nominated in that category, but Heath Ledger received a posthumous Oscar for his extraordinary performance). Nolan's example showed that serious actors need not fear signing up for a superhero movie and that the presence of Batmobiles and pointy ears need not be synonymous with even a small degree of camp. His Batman reshaped Hollywood and taught superhero films to aim higher, and for that he deserves respect.

THE IRON MAN TRILOGY

"SOMETIMES, YOU GOTTA RUN BEFORE YOU CAN WALK," SAYS TONY STARK, AS HE PERFECTS HIS IRON MAN SUIT. HE COULD EASILY BE DESCRIBING MARVEL'S APPROACH TO THIS FIRST FILM IN THEIR CINEMATIC UNIVERSE. IT'S SUCH CONFIDENT STORYTELLING, AND SUCH A FULLY REALIZED CHARACTER, THAT YOU'D BE FORGIVEN FOR THINKING THEY WERE 20 FILMS IN AND WELL ESTABLISHED, RATHER THAN LAUNCHING ONE OF THE RISKIEST VENTURES IN BLOCKBUSTER-FILMMAKING HISTORY.

We open with silence, a desert, Humvees (both humdrum-vees and fun-vees) before AC/DC's "Back in Black" drops and Robert Downey Jr's Tony Stark sips a whisky from a crystal glass. This guy, it's clear, may be in or near an active war zone, but that's no reason not to have fun. Disaster strikes – but before we see the consequences of that attack, we flash back to see Tony's carefree existence as a genius billionaire playboy philanthropist. He is supremely unreliable, terminally irresponsible and extremely impressed with his own cleverness. But there's a good heart underneath the narcissism – something that becomes steadily clearer through this series.

Tony is injured and captured by a terrorist group called the Ten Rings (a name that comics fans will instantly associate with the Mandarin). Forced to make weapons for them, he and his fellow captive, Yinsen (Shaun Toub), instead make a tiny "arc reactor" to keep the shrapnel in his body from his heart, and then use its excess energy to power a heavy iron suit that allows Tony to escape – though Yinsen sacrifices his life to get his friend out. It's a hell of a beginning, and enough to explain why a formerly callow man might start to think more deeply about the world. Which, of course, he does. But first, there's tinkering

to be done (by *Infinity War*, his suit is on its fiftieth incarnation and is entirely made of nano-bots) and limits to be broken.

Above The cast of *Iron Man* face up: Robert Downey Jr, Gwyneth Paltrow, Jeff Bridges and Terrence Howard.

Opposite Key art from *Iron Man 3*, with Stark facing the destruction of his whole lifestyle.

It's notable that when Iron Man first goes into action, it's to protect people like Yinsen. His attack on the terrorists of Gomira is foreign-policy wish fulfilment at its finest; clearly delineated good and bad guys, and a situation where a carefully applied use of force can save lives. Back home, however, things are less clear, with Tony's right-hand man, Obadiah Stane (Jeff Bridges as the best-named character in comics), working to undermine him and eventually armouring up as Ironmonger to take him down. It takes quick thinking by Gwyneth Paltrow's Pepper Potts, Tony's assistant, to get the evidence of his illegal arms dealing to S.H.I.E.L.D. and help save the day.

The film's final scene, in which Tony calls a press conference to present his elaborate alibi, cements the MCU attitude to superhero movies. Tony decides almost immediately to ditch the charade and declare himself as Iron Man. Except possibly for spies and the under-18s, the MCU has no time for secret identities: its heroes would be "out", opening up a whole heap of potential problems.

Some of those problems crop up in *Iron Man 2*.

First, Mickey Rourke's Ivan Vanko/Whiplash attacks Tony at the Monaco Grand Prix, forcing Tony to don his stylish and practical briefcase armour (the Mark V) and defeat him. Then Vanko's broken out of jail by rival arms manufacturer Justin Hammer (Sam Rockwell, playing stupid enough to be dangerous). That unholy alliance largely plays out in the background while Tony fails to cope with the fact that his reactor is poisoning him. His best friend, Colonel James "Rhodey" Rhodes (Don Cheadle, taking over from the first film's Terrence Howard), dons his armour against a drunk and uncontrolled Iron Man when the acting out gets out of control. "You wanna be a war machine, then take your shot," dares Tony.

Opposite, left Don Cheadle's Rhodey / War Machine, back-to-back with Iron Man in the second film's finale

Opposite, right Gwyneth Paltrow's Pepper Potts is far more than just Tony's love interest.

Below Scarlett Johansson as Natasha 'Black Widow' Romanov.

Rhodey takes the advice, and the name.

This one is the lesser, stand-alone *Iron Man*. There's heavy world-building to do, establishing more facts about S.H.I.E.L.D. (Clark Gregg's Agent Coulson is a fan of *Supernanny*!), introducing Scarlett Johansson's Natasha "Black Widow" Romanov, developing Tony and Pepper's romance, and making repeated references to the incident in the "south-west region" (Thor's arrival). Still, it has one of the best Marvel soundtracks and an enjoyably preposterous approach to science: it's never enough that Tony does science; he also has to flex his muscles in a vest at the same time. By the time he and Rhodey face off against another big, stupid-looking version of his Iron Man suit, you'll be entertained despite yourself.

That was director Jon Favreau's last film in the franchise, but Shane Black was no downgrade. He'd directed Downey before, on *Kiss Kiss Bang Bang*, and his rhythms of speech suited the star perfectly. He also leaned in to the post-traumatic stress that followed Tony's near-death experience in *Avengers*, taking him – mentally at least – back to that cave in Afghanistan. This one takes some risks, with Tony isolated and attacked by the nefarious pairing of Guy Pearce's scientist, Aldrich Killian – another dark reflection of Tony's past – and Sir Ben Kingsley's shadowy terrorist, the Mandarin. Or is he? As it turns out, Kingsley is an addled actor named Trevor Slattery ("They say his

Lear was the toast of Croydon, wherever that is") and not the real Mandarin at all. It's a cute twist that no one saw coming, and a way to get around the sad fact that the comics' version now looks like a dated and rather racist stereotype.

This is a very funny film ("Honestly, I hate working here. They're so weird," says one goon when Tony threatens him) and boasts one of the all-time great kid sidekicks in Ty Simpkins' Harley. But it also has really traumatic moments: the suit's attack on Pepper guided by Tony's subconscious, the Hollywood explosion in which Happy is injured, the destruction of Tony's mansion. It's to Shane Black and Robert Downey's credit that they keep the tone dancing on the line between comedy and tragedy, finally rebuilding Tony Stark into a slightly healthier guy.

Tony would, of course, have more challenges to overcome. His trauma-fuelled mania for safety and security would lead to devastation in *Age of Ultron* and the controversial Sokovia Accords. He would keep fighting to keep Earth safe; in fact, that would become his mission. Howard Stark's philosophy, as quoted by Tony, was that "Peace means having a bigger stick than the other guy." Since he went into that cave, Tony Stark has spent his life trying to ensure that he always has the bigger stick, to protect the people he loves. Long may the one-man nuclear deterrent reign.

THE MARVEL CINEMATIC UNIVERSE

HERE ARE THE FILMS – SO FAR – THAT MAKE UP MARVEL'S VAST, INTERLINKED MOVIE UNIVERSE.

The run of Marvel films from *Iron Man* in 2008 to *Avengers: Endgame* in 2019 is entirely unparalleled in cinema history: 22 interlocked films, almost all of them at least good (ahem, *Iron Man 2* and *The Dark World*…), building to a series of crossover climaxes in the Avengers films that punctuate the run. The series is insanely ambitious and astonishingly successful, despite a huge disparity in topic and tone running from the 1970s political-thriller style of *The Winter Soldier* to the space comedy of *Guardians of the Galaxy*. If people seem unreasonably devoted to the MCU, it's a love that has been earned with gripping storytelling and likeable characters. It's basically now the world's biggest-budget soap opera, but with better effects.

Key to the whole operation is Kevin Feige, president of Marvel Studios and the guiding hand behind the whole operation. Feige was an associate producer on the first X-Men film and many of the films that followed, but he really came into his own as president of production at the newly established Marvel Studios in 2007. What followed was a grand experiment: five superhero franchises building to the first *Avengers*, and a shared universe that spread its tentacles from there. Here are the films that make up the series so far.

PHASE ONE

| IRON MAN (2008) | THE INCREDIBLE HULK (2008) | IRON MAN 2 (2010) | THOR (2011) | CAPTAIN AMERICA: THE FIRST AVENGER (2011) | MARVEL'S THE AVENGERS (2012) |

PHASE TWO

IRON MAN 3
(2013)

THOR: THE DARK
WORLD (2013)

CAPTAIN AMERICA:
THE WINTER SOLDIER
(2014)

GUARDIANS OF
THE GALAXY (2014)

AVENGERS: AGE OF
ULTRON (2015)

ANT-MAN
(2015)

PHASE THREE

CAPTAIN AMERICA:
CIVIL WAR (2016)

DOCTOR STRANGE
(2016)

GUARDIANS OF THE
GALAXY VOL. 2 (2017)

SPIDER-MAN:
HOMECOMING (2017)

THOR: RAGNAROK
(2017)

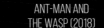

BLACK PANTHER
(2018)

AVENGERS: INFINITY
WAR (2018)

ANT-MAN AND
THE WASP (2018)

CAPTAIN MARVEL
(2019)

AVENGERS: ENDGAME
(2019)

WATCHMEN

IT'S THE HOLY GRAIL OF GRAPHIC NOVELS, THE CITIZEN KANE OF THE GENRE, AND IT DEFIED FILMMAKERS FOR OVER 20 YEARS.

Alan Moore and Dave Gibbons' limited series imagined a dystopian world in which superheroes and costumed vigilantes once operated but are now outlawed, but it's also a biting and multi-layered satire on Thatcherite Britain, nuclear terror and all the ways that humanity screws up the world, with interlinked alt-history meanderings and a story about a comic-book pirate woven into the whole. Good luck boiling *that* down to a tidy feature running time. And yet Zack Snyder and his team finally met the challenge. If it didn't satisfy everyone, at least no one could accuse him of taking the subject matter lightly.

Not that it was a foregone conclusion that it would be the director who made such a success of Frank Miller's *300* who got to tackle this. *Watchmen* had gone through several studios, some of them multiple times. Michael Bay was mooted, Darren Aronofsky came close, while Paul Greengrass had cast his leads and designed his sets before his funding fell apart in 2005. A few months later, it went back to Warners and Snyder came aboard. When offered the chance, he worried that he might fail the novel he admired so much, but figured that, if he passed and someone else blew it the failure would still be his responsibility for turning it down. So Snyder, as with *300*, took the graphic novel as his lodestone and stuck with the story he knew should work, sometimes even using Gibbons' frames as a storyboard. The colour scheme echoes the comics too: greens and purples dominate; colours like a bruise, like illness.

When casting, Snyder turned to relatively fresh faces, the better to disappear into the characters –

literally disappear, in the case of Billy Crudup's blue CG Doctor Manhattan. Patrick Wilson, Matthew Goode, Jeffrey Dean Morgan and Malin Akerman got big career boosts as Nite Owl II, Ozymandias, the Comedian and Silk Spectre II. But the film's casting masterstroke was Jackie Earle Haley as Rorschach, the most uncompromising of the Watchmen and the only one whose real name not even his teammates know. Haley's snarling, nihilistic and blackly funny diaries provide the film's narration and translate the feel of the book superbly.

The form, too, adheres closely to the comic. We open with the murder of the Comedian, and

Above The 'original' Watchmen group of superheroes, in a photo closely modelled on one in Alan Moore and Dave Gibbons' comic.

Opposite The film's poster art sold the dark tone.

Rorschach worried that the rest of his former teammates could be at risk. As he visits each one to warn them of a killer, he gradually realizes that something else might really be afoot – but what? It is 1984: nuclear war is threatening and an energy crisis looms. Meanwhile, the only truly superpowered being on the planet, Doctor Manhattan, is distracted from his attempts to solve that crisis by a string of personal scandals and his failing relationship with Akerman's Laurie. But how, if at all, are these things connected? Rorschach is paranoid, but maybe someone is also out to get him.

It's about mood and character more than plot: the mood is gloomy and the characters morose, but they're both beautifully developed over a running time that was generous even before Snyder's director's cut. Snyder layers in the flashbacks to the older generation of heroes, with Carla Gugino particularly good as the first Silk Spectre, and builds in all the texture he can. That remarkable fidelity to the source meant there was little for fans to complain about: even Snyder's changes to the ending passed muster, streamlining the story considerably and avoiding its more *outré* elements. Then again, that was also the principal and most lasting criticism: the film's very fidelity means that it verges on plodding, with few of the inspired leaps and apparent non-sequiturs that so enlivened Moore and Gibbons' work in the first place.

Then again, Snyder's eye does give the film moments of greatness. The opening montage, laying out the alternative history that brings us to the 1984 of the book to the strains of Bob Dylan's "The Times They Are A-Changing", is beautiful, visual storytelling at its finest. Maybe if Snyder had trusted his story sense as much as his eye for a visual and felt freer to venture away from the text, this could have connected more deeply with audiences, as the book did. More likely, it was never particularly well suited to becoming a blockbuster. Watchmen's film, like its book, remains defiantly different from everything around it; something unique in a sea of shinier, more optimistic heroes. Sometimes, it's good to confront the darkness.

Top Billy Crudup as the godlike Doctor Manhattan, the only true superhero of the lot.

Above Malin Akerman as Silk Spectre II, rescuing people from a burning building.

Opposite Nite Owl (Patrick Wilson) II fights his way through a prison riot.

V FOR VENDETTA

Another adaptation of an Alan Moore (and David Lloyd) book, this sees a fascist England brought down by a masked freedom fighter named V (Hugo Weaving), with the help of a young office worker named Evie (Natalie Portman). Together, they attack the leading figures of the state and plan a new gunpowder plot. Directed by James McTeigue and produced by the Wachowskis, this is a pretty faithful adaptation and one that maintains the downbeat tone and rainy atmosphere of the comics. What's more, Portman is great, and the revelations of V's motivations and background give his story a poignancy and righteous fury that few heroes can match. Remember, remember, the 5th of November.

SCOTT PILGRIM VS. THE WORLD

IT'S DEFINITELY BASED ON A COMIC BOOK (BRYAN LEE O'MALLEY'S GENIUS SERIES), AND SUPERHEROIC THINGS HAPPEN IN IT, BUT EDGAR WRIGHT'S *SCOTT PILGRIM VS. THE WORLD* IS UNLIKE ANY OTHER FILM IN THIS BOOK.

This is not about deciding what to do with one's superpowers or taking up a career as a crime fighter. It's actually more of a romantic epic with fight scenes. The spectacular battles and outlandish twists into unreality are – honestly – just a metaphor for life and dating in your early twenties, when everything seems a little vague and unformed until someone or something suddenly snaps into focus.

The plot is your typical boy-meets-girl story. Scott Pilgrim (Michael Cera) falls for Ramona Flowers (Mary Elizabeth Winstead) after she takes a sub-space shortcut through his head to make her Amazon deliveries. But for them to be happy together, he must break up with his adorable girlfriend, Knives (Ellen Wong), and, oh yes, defeat Ramona's seven evil exes in mortal combat. As if that weren't enough, Scott's evil ex, Envy Adams (Brie Larson), comes back into town, and there's a Battle of the Bands to win.

Opposite Slacker Scott Pilgrim (Michael Cera) shreds on bass with his band Sex-Bob-Omb.

Below Ramona Flowers (Mary Elizabeth Winstead) is the object of Scott's affection and a formidable fighter.

These characters all live in a world of band practices and house parties, and have menial jobs if they have jobs at all. "My last job was a long story filled with sighs," says Scott of his own CV; he's so penniless that he needs his high-school girlfriend to pay for their dates in the arcade. It's a portrait of the kind of Generation X slacker lifestyle that has largely disappeared for the harder-working millennial cohort, but it allows space for, well, epic combat, and that's the fun of the thing. And also disappointing garage-band music. Scott's introduction on behalf of his band is, "We are Sex Bob-Omb and we're here to make you think about death and get sad and stuff!"

The language and much of the logic (if that's the word) of the story comes from video games and anime, rather than simply comics. Battles are announced like *Street Fighter*; the defeated parties explode into clouds of coins; characters can float in the air or create vast creature avatars. Still, Wright preserves the feel of the

Above Scott battles final boss Gideon Graves (Jason Schwartzman) for Ramona.

Opposite Scott, Ramona, Young Neil (Johnny Simmons), Knives, Kim Pine (Alison Pill) and Stephen Stills (Mark Webber).

graphic novel too, shifting fluidly from panel to panel and adding helpful or amusing captions throughout. Flashbacks take place in illustrations drawn directly from Bryan Lee O'Malley's graphics, which also serve as game icons in some of Scott's fights. Wright's long-standing propensity for quick, precise cutting fits perfectly with the subject matter, and keeps the pace moving astonishingly fast. It helps us keep up with the quick and only vaguely logical leaps of Scott's thought processes, because the cinematic language is so beautifully on the button. Wright also has an incredible eye for casting, filling his film with people who could, and often soon would, be superheroes. To give you an idea of how appropriately superheroic this lot are, the line-up includes the once or future Superman, Captain America, Captain Marvel, LEGO Robin, Royal Pain, Human Torch, Punisher and The Atom.

And then there are the battle scenes. The hapless Scott must take on dancing pirate Matthew Patel (Satya Bhabha) and skateboarding action-movie star Lucas Lee (Chris Evans as an hilariously preening A-list monster). Then there's superpowered vegan bassist Todd Ingram (Brandon Routh, also sending up his clean-cut image), "bi-furious" Roxy Richter (Mae Whitman) and the Katayanagi twins (Shota and Keita Saito) before he reaches the boss level: Jason Schwartzman's seductive, controlling, deeply weird Gideon Graves.

The jokes are layered endlessly, some of them so quick you'll need a re-watch and a pause button to catch them. But there's substance here underneath. Scott has to help Ramona escape from a string of bad decisions and one domineering ex in particular; he also needs to confront his own demons and grow up. He is, after all, a 22-year-old so hapless that he shares the bed of his studio apartment with a friend because he can't pay his own rent.

The film's biggest flaw is that Scott doesn't really seem good enough for either of his girlfriends and, arguably, he ends up with the wrong one (O'Malley's books, which were not finished at the time of the film, went in a slightly different direction). But he's likeable in his hopelessness, and seems set on a brighter path (literally) by the end. Still, he is unlike any other superhero in this book in that he's deeply, defiantly ordinary and a bit ineffectual, apart from his fighting skills. There's something wonderful about that. This film says that our own tiny struggles to win someone's heart, or to forge a relationship despite all our emotional baggage, are acts of superheroism in their own right, and that is an inspiring thought.

THE THOR TRILOGY

IT'S AN ODD COINCIDENCE THAT THE TWO SPOILED RICH BOYS OF THE AVENGERS UNIVERSE – THE GUYS WITH FATHER COMPLEXES TO BURN – ALSO SHARE THE SAME PATTERN TO THEIR FILMS. THERE'S THE SOLID FIRST EFFORT, THE WEAK FOLLOW-UP WITH JUST A FEW GREAT MOMENTS, AND A RISKY, TONALLY DIFFERENT THIRD OUTING THAT LEANS INTO THE LEADING MAN'S STRENGTHS AND SMASHES IT OUT OF THE PARK. AND ARGUABLY, WHEN THOR HIT HIS STRIDE HE DID SO IN EVEN MORE SPECTACULAR FASHION THAN IRON MAN.

It's worth remembering how big a risk this seemed at the beginning. In the relatively grounded world of Iron Man and even the Hulk, how does a god from an alien world fit in? Marvel answered by hiring Shakespeare stalwart Kenneth Branagh to direct, and by leaning into Thor's otherness, giving us a fish-out-of-water story that was so charming we forgot to reject wilder concepts like the rainbow bridge and an eight-legged horse called Sleipnir. Thor told us that his people saw no real difference between science and magic, and we all just shrugged and bought it. After all, who's going to argue with the guy whose muscles have muscles?

Branagh's casting, importantly, was also spotless. Anthony Hopkins is a worn but still authoritative Odin; Idris Elba an otherworldly Heimdall, and British newcomer Tom Hiddleston an impish, smarty-pants Loki. Chris Hemsworth, as Thor himself, looked the part, but more importantly, he had the jockish amiability to make us care about a Viking-looking bruiser. Even in that first film, he showed a light touch in the few comic moments he got amid his exile angst. His flirtation with Natalie Portman's serious physicist, Jane, is cute: she's discombobulated by his sheer size and professionally fascinated by

Above Chris Hemsworth's Thor with brother Loki (Tom Hiddleston).

Opposite Hemsworth looks every bit the Norse god.

his existence; he loves her for her mind. Most of the finale, unusually for Marvel, keeps things small and intimate: a family feud in a dusty Western town during which Loki, characteristically, handles the fighting by proxy.

For a film with so much comedy, however – bolstered further by Jamie Alexander's Sif and the Warriors Three, as well as Jane's intern, Darcy – it ends on a bummer. Thor destroys the Rainbow Bridge to save the Nine Realms, cutting himself off from Jane, while Loki falls into the void.

The Dark World picks up two years later, after Thor has fought his father's domain back into line and, incidentally, reclaimed Loki in 2012's *Avengers*. Crucially, however, he has failed to make it back to Earth for a date with Jane during that time. But when Christopher Eccleston's Malekith, his Dark Elves and a galatic Convergence threaten, they meet again and save Greenwich from becoming the flashpoint of a cataclysm. It's a messier and less focused film, with the action shifting to Asgard halfway through just so we can learn about the nature of Infinity Stones and discover that Marvel planned thriftily to turn five films' worth of McGuffins into one mega-McGuffin, the *Infinity Gauntlet* (*see Avengers: Infinity War*). Newly appointed director Alan Taylor knew high fantasy, but he had significant reshoots and rewrites to the ending, so there's a lingering lack of conviction in places. The Loki and Thor show still entertains, and Portman gets to show her comic gifts occasionally as Jane, but it's the poor relation of the three films.

Third time lucky, however. Taika Waititi picked up the hammer and emphatically proved that he was worthy of the power of Thor. The New Zealand director, fresh from comic masterpiece *Hunt for the Wilderpeople*, realized three fundamental facts at the exact same time. One, Hemsworth was a far better comedian than he had so far been able to showcase in the role – look at his work on *Ghostbusters* or in the *Vacation* remake. Two, the Loki story was played out and his constant double-crosses risked becoming tiresome. And three, this series needed more Led Zeppelin. A lot more.

Ragnarok was, accordingly, a glam-rock gonzo delight as Thor loses everything to his goddess-of-

Top Tessa Thompson's fearsome Valkyrie cuts a path through her enemies.

Above Idris Elba as Asgard's gatekeeper and Thor's BFF Heimdall.

Opposite Hela faces off with the forces of Asgard in one of Ragnarok's most exquisite shots.

Overleaf Thor faces off with the incredible Hulk. Brace for impact.

death sister, Hela (Cate Blanchett), and finds himself forced to engage in gladiatorial combat with the Hulk (Mark Ruffalo). He makes new allies in Valkyrie (Tessa Thompson), a rock monster called Korg (Waititi) and Loki (sort of), and doesn't go near Earth at all. Jeff Goldblum turns up as an Eternal – a being millions of years old (probably) called the Grandmaster – and that makes complete sense and perhaps finally explains how Jeff Goldblum has stayed magical all these years. This is a superhero movie played out like a wild 1980s fantasy, filled with power chords and electronica. But where those films had shonky effects and embarrassing performances, for the most part, this is coming down with acting talent, and has the mega-budget of a modern blockbuster to allow for some really dazzling effects. You'll believe a man can fight a Hulk.

That brawl is a tie, of course, but it's not as if the film otherwise lacks the courage of its convictions,

destroying Asgard quite emphatically and saying goodbye to Odin. Hela simply wipes out the Warriors Three, who had been treated as an afterthought since the first film, and takes one of Thor's eyes for good measure. We should really never have doubted that Cate Blanchett would be a formidable bad guy, but the revelation of her existence rather surprisingly proves that Thor is the odd one out in his family: his mother was a witch, his father a warlord, and his siblings are Goth drama queens with too much gel in their hair.

It's a film with a huge body count, and yet it's riotous and reckless and a complete delight to watch. As the rest of the original Avengers approached what we feared would be their finale with *Infinity War* and *Endgame*, it suddenly seemed that Thor might be the one we'd miss the most. There's always room for a barmy superhero film that features a space phenomenon called the Devil's Anus, after all, and Thor had only just hit his stride.

THE CAPTAIN AMERICA TRILOGY

SUPERHERO ORIGIN STORIES TYPICALLY SEE AN AVERAGE PERSON GIVEN

EXTRAORDINARY GIFTS, BUT FEW START OFF AS DISADVANTAGED AS STEVE ROGERS.

A SCRAWNY KID SUFFERING FROM EVERY CHRONIC AILMENT GOING, HE IS SO

PATENTLY UNFIT THAT HE CANNOT GET DRAFTED INTO THE US ARMY – EVEN

IN WARTIME.

However far he goes as Captain America, across two eras and facing space scumbags unlike anything he could have dreamed of, underneath he's still a little guy. He's still someone who just doesn't like bullies. That scrawny pipsqueak is the ultimate wellspring of his irresistible moral force and the reason that he slowly became the central gravity of the Avengers when the outer skin came to reflect his inner strength. In other words, the MCU's most consistent trilogy relies on character.

It is significant that we never see Chris Evans' Steve Rogers actively volunteer for the procedure that makes him a "super-soldier". We see why other people choose him for the programme: he would throw himself on a grenade for others, he's intelligent, he's considerate – and he's small enough that the procedure's effectiveness will never be doubted. Tommy Lee Jones' Colonel Phillips, head of the programme, is reluctantly convinced to use him as a test subject; idealistic scientist Dr Erskine (Stanley Tucci) is rather more enthusiastic. We eventually see Steven demand that they keep the procedure going even when he's in agony – but we never see him actively choose to change. His enhanced abilities are something that he accepts out of duty, rather than seeking due to some lust for power. Steve doesn't need super-muscles to stand up to bullies; he's been doing it forever.

Steve Rogers was orphaned young, and grew up stoical and self-contained, despite the best efforts of his bosom buddy, Bucky (Sebastian Stan). However, as a soldier he found ways to work with a team. Against the worst Nazi threats of World War II alongside the Howling Commandos and, after his accidental cryogenic freezing, with the Avengers, Steve Rogers demonstrated a knack for leadership that even Thor and Tony Stark couldn't deny and didn't particularly challenge. Give him a serious threat and you find a serious guy. Yet those who have known him longest – Bucky and Peggy (Hayley Atwell) – sometimes accuse him of dramatic tendencies (he was an art student in the comics) and treat him like a slightly chaotic force. That erratic behaviour isn't a lack of care, however, but a surfeit of it: what drives Steve to act unpredictably is a superhuman faith in his own belief system and an absolute determination to do right.

The experiment that made him was designed to produce perfect soldiers; men who go where they are told and fight whoever they find there. But Steve Rogers follows his own code and that is, in military terms, far from ideal. Sometimes that means he plays the system, as in *The First Avenger* when, exhausted, he out-thinks the commands of a barking drill sergeant to

Opposite Chris Evans in his best (to date) comic book role as Steve Rogers / Captain America.

cadge a ride back to camp. But he will smash the rules when necessary, ignoring orders to single-handedly save nearly 400 POWs from the Nazi HYDRA division. He surrenders himself to Colonel Phillips for discipline immediately afterward, but the fact that he does so in front of his hundreds of rescuees suggests more sneakiness than those who dismiss him as a goody-good would admit. This man respects authority to a point, but he will always decide for himself. More importantly, he also respects those without power and authority.

Steve Rogers' rebelliousness was developed more fully across his own two sequels. In *The Winter Soldier*, Steve went to war against his own employer, the superhero-oversight/spy organization, S.H.I.E.L.D., when he learned that it had been infiltrated by HYDRA. Along the way he also took time to throw shade at US foreign policy post 9/11 ("This isn't freedom, this is fear") because this Captain America stands not for what the politicians say America is, but what the US *should* be.

In *Civil War*, he took up arms against, well, *everyone* in order to maintain his independence of conscience and then, in defence of Bucky – now a HYDRA-brainwashed assassin with a metal arm. Steve has seen what it looks like to blindly follow orders and isn't willing to do so again; it's an interesting contrast to Bucky's brainwashed inability to deny the orders he's given as well. Steve is fighting to free himself and his friend, to finally end their World War II service. The genius of these two Russo brothers-directed *Captain America* sequels has been to put Steve Rogers in a situation painted entirely in shades of uncertainty and then leave him to try to figure out the right thing to do. Sometimes

Opposite, top Peggy Carter (Hayley Atwell) leads World War II troops in an assault on a Hydra base.

Opposite, bottom Bucky Barnes (Sebastian Stan) returns as the brainwashed Winter Soldier in the second film.

Below Scarlett Johansson's Black Widow becomes Steve's sidekick in *The Winter Soldier*.

that turns out to be tearing down part of America's security apparatus. Sometimes it's fighting his own friends to save a (strictly speaking) innocent life. He may be sure in his judgement of right and wrong, but that conviction doesn't ever make his life easy. The freedom he stands for comes with responsibility – an almost impossible onus to do good.

Behind the scenes, *Captain America* has the huge advantage that, of his seven major MCU roles (not counting the fun cameos in *The Dark World* and *Homecoming*), five came from the same writing team. Screenwriters Christopher Marcus and Steven

McFeeley have seen him through all three of his own films and his latter two *Avengers* movies, and it shows in a remarkably consistent character arc (the other two came from Joss Whedon, who also knows what's what). Small moments in *The First Avenger* (a Spielbergian pleasure that's easily the MCU's most underrated film, and one of its most re-watchable) came to feed gracefully into big parts of its excellent sequels.

We know instinctively now who Cap is, though, like Bucky and Peggy, we *still* don't always know how he'll react. But we can trust that it will usually be for the best. Far from being the goody-good of the MCU, Captain America has quietly become its most complex character, someone who will not just stand up for what's right but also take the time and consideration to figure out what "right" looks like. And he could do it all day.

Top Lines are drawn that split the Avengers down the middle in *Civil War*.

Opposite Team Steve vs. Team Tony: whose side are you on?

X-MEN: FIRST CLASS AND DAYS OF FUTURE PAST

AFTER *X-MEN: THE LAST STAND* FINISHED THAT TRILOGY ON A SLIGHTLY BUM NOTE, 20TH CENTURY FOX LOOKED FOR WAYS TO RELAUNCH THE *X-MEN* SAGA. THE SOLUTION? BRING IN COOL BRITISH DIRECTOR MATTHEW VAUGHN TO TAKE IT IN A RADICAL NEW DIRECTION.

The idea was to take the X-Men back to the decade in which they were created and lean into the 1960s aesthetic with go-go dancers, Bond-esque spy capering and some very groovy mutations, baby.

The setting may match the original X-books, but the line-up is a little different. In this reality, James McAvoy's young, playboy Charles Xavier has adopted Raven "Mystique" Darkholme (Jennifer Lawrence) as his sister. The pair are recruited by CIA Agent Moira McTaggart (Rose Byrne) to investigate apparent mutant activity by Sebastian Shaw (Kevin Bacon) and Emma Frost (January Jones). But the spanner in everyone's plans will prove to be Erik "Magneto" Lehnsherr (Michael Fassbender), who is determined to get his revenge on Shaw and secure a future for mutantkind.

Vaughn boldly recreates that Auschwitz-set opening scene to the first *X-Men* to establish Erik's past with Shaw, and his story unfolds as a quietly violent revenge thriller as he tracks down Nazis and their enablers around the world. In comparison, the privileged Xavier – long-haired and not yet in a wheelchair – has had it easy, hitting on every pretty girl around Oxford and blithely laughing off Mystique's concerns about the prejudice against mutants that means she must mask her natural blue appearance. Still, there's a meeting of minds between Erik and Charles, an almost-romance sense of connection and complementary powers. Maybe these two crazy kids can work things out!

Or, well, maybe not. The finale is cleverly timed to the Cuban Missile Crisis, but in the course of averting nuclear war, Erik takes up Shaw's telepathy-blocking helmet. It's a sign, both literally and metaphorically, that he is adopting part of Shaw's mantle and cutting himself off from the peaceful co-existence that Charles advocates. And Mystique, as fate dictates she must, goes off with Magneto to wage a guerrilla war for mutant rights as Charles is left with a bullet in his spine and no feeling in his legs.

The sequel, in terms of those characters, resets things slightly. It's now 1973, but Charles is walking about again – though he sacrifices his powers to do it. Once again there is a battle for Mystique's soul, and a wild-card element in Erik's behaviour. But the stroke of genius is to unite both generations of X-Men in a retelling of the classic Chris Claremont story *Days of Future Past*. We start in a dystopian future where Sentinels – robots created to destroy mutants – have evolved rapidly to counter any and all mutant abilities and laid waste to much of the planet. In this *Terminator*-esque hellscape, a young

Opposite Telepath Charles Xavier (James McAvoy) and metal-manipulator Erik Lehnsherr (Michael Fassbender) meet and become BFFs. That'll last.

cadre of mutants and former X-students reunite with Professor X, Magneto, Wolverine and Storm to send Wolverine's consciousness back in time and stop a Mystique assassination before it happens. The time traveller is different from the one in the comic – there, it was Kitty Pryde who slipped along the time stream – but at least the assassin remains the same. And the film's wrinkle that it's Mystique's shape-shifting DNA that is key to the Sentinels' abilities.

The shifting timeline allows for neat gags like a pre-*Project X* Wolverine going through a metal detector and *not* setting it off, or a Sentinel turning to Emma Frost-style diamond to resist a fiery blast. And the high stakes of the future timeline balance the lighter moments of 1970s disco or Nixon impersonation. That half of the time also gives us some upsetting scenes. Halle Berry's Storm gets one great moment and is then ignominiously killed – in line with her shabby treatment throughout her four *X*-films. It's upsetting to see the X-Men apparently picked off one by one in both past and future, and to see Magneto and Mystique once again flirt with the line between right and wrong. Ultimately, the biggest flaw of *Days*

Above Magneto takes flight in a show of raw power.

Opposite, top Quicksilver (Evan Peters) joins an X-Men prison break. Cue a stellar, slow-mo scene.

Opposite, left James McAvoy begins to take on the iconic Professor X look.

of Future Past is that it does not significantly advance the 1970s line-up. Once again, Charles has gained a measure of serenity and set up a school. Once again, Erik has gone to ground. The biggest change is that Mystique walks away from both, in search of her own destiny.

The ending for the future timeline, however, is cheerier – in fact, it was privately dubbed the "happy mansion" scene by the cast and crew. All the mistakes of *X3* are undone, so that Scott and Jean are alive and well, Kelsey Grammar is back as Beast, the school is thriving and even Logan is a more contented soul than he was before. It's an idealized finale, sure, but it's also enormously satisfying for fans to see these put-upon outsiders in a place of safety and contentment for once. Everyone deserves a good day now and again.

X-MEN: APOCALYPSE

Here's a film derailed by its own good casting. By *Apocalypse*, Jennifer Lawrence became one of the world's biggest stars and so Mystique had to become a force for good and even an X-leader. But it once again feels like no one has progressed in the decade since the last film. Xavier is still moping. Magneto is motivated by the single most hackneyed device in super-storytelling: the death of his wife and daughter. When he then destroys a city, everyone worries about his redemption but not the millions he must have killed. Oscar Isaac, as bald, blue, uber-bad Apocalypse, suggests that his power to convince depends, Samson-like, on his hair. About the only bright spark is Kodi Smit-McPhee's teenage Nightcrawler, and his adorable Flock of Seagulls hair and "Thriller" jacket.

THE AVENGERS AND AVENGERS: AGE OF ULTRON

IT'S DIFFICULT TO MAKE A FILM WITH A LOT OF MOVING PARTS, WHICH IS ONE

REASON WHY MANY FIRST-TIME DIRECTORS CHOOSE A SMALL, CONTAINED STORY.

But it is exponentially harder when you are uniting the stars of four or more franchises, each with their own tone and priorities, each with an in-demand star, and each of which could be damaged or derailed by a bad crossover film. That's why, in the strictest sense of the word, the first *Avengers* movie is an experimental film. It's also why the success of any of them is sort of miraculous.

Really, it could have failed. No one outside Marvel knew if the high fantasy of *Thor* would play against the sci-fi tech of Tony Stark or the old-fashioned heroics of *Captain America*. No one much liked *Hulk*, if you can remember those distant times. But the careful preparation and dependable casting (or, if necessary, recasting) of the MCU made it work.

It helped to have Joss Whedon, a master of group

dynamics, genre-bending and snappy dialogue, in charge. It helped, too, that the Avengers were so phenomenally well cast (or, in the case of Bruce Banner, recast). There was no sense that certain stars had demanded more screen time or better lines as their price for appearing. Perhaps they trusted that Whedon would do right by them all in his story, and they must quickly have realized that there were no bad lines at all.

So the team bicker, brawl and come reluctantly together to beat Tom Hiddleston's Loki and a Chitauri

Opposite Iron Man and Captain America face off against the James Spader-voiced Ultron.

Below The iconic Avengers line-up that would define the first two Phases of the MCU.

army. Captain America, perhaps surprisingly, emerges as team leader amid the chaos, with Tony Stark ceding the strategy to the more experienced soldier. Then again, Iron Man made the key play so he didn't exactly lack for glory. But it still demonstrates a commendable (and consistent) dedication to story over star-power. It would have been easy to have the more established, better known Downey as our principal hero with everyone else merely huddled around his repulsors – but it would give Cap relatively little to do, and leave the team lacking his moral authority.

What's glorious about it is how well everyone bounces off one another, how natural the interplay feels. Of course, Cap and Tony would butt heads, even while feeling a wary, Howard Stark-fuelled kinship underneath. Of course, Hulk would be the one thing who could shake Black Widow's composure. And of course, Hawkeye would overcome his brainwashing and give us some of the coolest shots of the film.

Literally. The action scenes are almost an unwelcome distraction from the gang just hanging out; you would quite happily watch these people just have a dinner party. Luckily, however, the banter continues through the action ("Make a move, Reindeer Games"; "That's not a party..."; "I'm always angry"; "Puny god") and the action is mostly terrific, from the three-way Cap/Thor/Tony custody battle for an imprisoned Loki to the New York smackdown finale. It's also pleasing to see a film in which collateral damage is treated as a problem: Cap spends as much time trying to quarantine the invaders and limit the destruction as he does personally dealing with alien menaces.

Luckily for the experiment, *Avengers* was a huge hit, and opened up the Marvel Universe for its "Phase

Opposite Tom Hiddleston's Loki stole the limelight as the Avengers' first major villain.

Below Cap and Thor team up to take down an alien invasion on the streets of New York.

Two", establishing a non-Asgard space civilization with its own warlords (ahead of *Guardians of the Galaxy*); shaking Tony's composure (ahead of the PTSD-themed *Iron Man 3*); telling Loki's story before *Thor: The Dark World*; and widening our access to S.H.I.E.L.D. ahead of *Captain America: The Winter Soldier* and, well, *Agents of S.H.I.E.L.D.*

The big crossover toward the end of Phase Two, *Age of Ultron*, was a slightly more muted affair. Occasionally in the MCU, the needs of the wider story require one film to set-up scenes or character for several more to come. Think of the S.H.I.E.L.D. subplot and the introduction of Black Widow in *Iron Man 2*, or the (more successful) integration of Spider-Man into *Civil War*. *Age of Ultron* got the gang back together, but used the reunion to establish story threads for much of Phase Three, including *Thor: Ragnarok*, *Civil War* and *Black Panther*. As such, it's a film doing a huge amount of heavy lifting for other films, and that sometimes distracts from the main plot.

That caveat aside, *Ultron* is better than it's sometimes given credit for. It seamlessly introduces two new antagonists/allies to the team in Scarlett Witch (Elizabeth Olsen) and Quicksilver (Aaron Taylor-Johnson), and gives us a chilling opponent in the James Spader-voiced Ultron, an AI who is no sooner created (more-or-less by Tony: oops) than he rejects all Asimov's laws of robotics and judges humanity unworthy of existence. Ultron and his mass-produced clones, laced with valuable and near-indestructible vibranium, plan to create an extinction-level event by launching a mass of the Earth's crust – one that happens to contain a city – into the stratosphere and then dropping it back down to create the same sort of devastating impact that wiped out the dinosaurs. The Avengers have to stop arguing (only partly fuelled by Scarlett Witch-inspired nightmares) long enough to stop him.

One key to stopping Ultron turns out to be the almost accidental creation of his perfected, more powerful opposite number, Paul Bettany's Vision. Bettany had been in the MCU since the beginning as the voice of Tony's home AI; now that AI, J.A.R.V.I.S., became a foundational ingredient in the

seraphic, red-faced Vision. After all the noise and chaos of that final battle, Vision finishes off the final, damaged Ultron clone in a quiet forest glade, with a philosophical discussion of humanity's strengths and weaknesses. It's the sort of grace note that makes these films more than just shoot-'em-ups, and creates fanatically devoted fans for these characters.

If *Avengers* showed that Marvel could take an immensely difficult task and make it look easy, *Age of Ultron*'s very faults allow us to see the frantic spinning of cogs and gears underneath. These gigantic crossovers are huge endeavours, and every time one succeeds it's the result of impressive, inspired creativity and extraordinarily detailed planning going hand-in-hand. It's not fair to dismiss these as cynical cash grabs (though they also make a lot of money); there's complex, multi-layered storytelling going on across these Phases and team-ups, and the scattering of failed cinematic universes that tried to follow Marvel's lead just shows how impressive their work is.

Top Elizabeth Olsen proved a powerful foe, and then an essential ally in Age of Ultron.

Opposite Iron Man dons the "Hulkbuster" armour to fight a Hulk driven to feral rage by Scarlet Witch's visions

BORN ON THE BIG SCREEN
THE SUPERHEROES ORIGINALLY CREATED FOR CINEMA

THIS BOOK FOCUSES ON COMIC-BOOK SUPERHEROES ADAPTED FOR FILM – BUT

WHAT ABOUT THOSE CREATED SOLELY FOR FEATURES? TIME TO GIVE THOSE

A CHANCE TO SHINE, AND SEE HOW THEY FARE COMPARED TO THE COMIC

ADAPTATIONS. IS IT REALLY EASIER TO WRITE SOMETHING DIRECTLY FOR THE SCREEN?

OR COULD SOME OF THESE HAVE DONE WITH A TRIAL RUN ON THE PAGE? WELL,

WITH MORE HITS THAN MISSES, HOLLYWOOD SCREENWRITERS MIGHT BE ABLE TO

GIVE THE COMIC-BOOK INDUSTRY A RUN FOR ITS MONEY.

THE INCREDIBLES AND INCREDIBLES 2

Pixar's superhero movie was a huge risk for the studio when it launched in 2004: it marked the first time they had animated large numbers of humans, and an exponentially bigger challenge than they had ever taken on previously. But the result was glorious. In a 1960s-inspired retro-future pastiche, superheroes have been banned from going into action and given cover identities in ordinary life. However, when Bob Parr/Mr Incredible goes back into action, he starts a chain of events that blows all their covers. The sequel, set minutes later, is also good – especially anything involving super-baby Jack-Jack – but the first one remains one of Pixar's most entertaining films, with one of its finest scores.

SKY HIGH

This charming mix of superhero film and high-school comedy stars Michael Angarano as Will Stronghold, the powerless son of the world's greatest superheroes. Exiled to his school's sidekicks programme (euphemistically dubbed "Hero Support") with the other under-performers, he eventually uncovers a plot and has to save the entire school. The underachiever-made-good is a familiar plot, but this brightly coloured comedy is bursting with positive messages for tweens, inspired in-jokes for adults (original Wonder Woman Lynda Carter plays the school's Principal Powers), and a plot not nearly as predictable as it looks. A good Superheroes 101 option.

SUPER

The film that landed James Gunn his *Guardians of the Galaxy* job is a violent look at what might happen if an ordinary guy (Rainn Wilson) set out to fight crime after losing his wife (Liv Tyler) to a blond-tipped lothario (Kevin Bacon). The basic notion of an indie superhero movie, defiantly lo-fi and often comic ("Shut up, crime!") is a great one, but this film goes to some *seriously* twisted places along the way. That's mostly thanks to Ellen Page's genuinely quite disturbing sidekick, who is like nothing you've ever seen before. Overshadowed by the similarly-themed *Kick-Ass* on release, it's become a cult favourite; Joss Whedon loved it so much he got Gunn into Marvel's orbit.

MY SUPER EX-GIRLFRIEND

Since seeing Kevin Smith's *Mall Rats*, if not before, people have wondered what it might be like to date a superhero. On this evidence, it's awful. Uma Thurman is the super-woman who dates with Luke Wilson's hapless architect, and makes his life a misery after he rejects her controlling behaviour. While we've all wanted to throw a shark at our ex (right?), so there's effective wish-fulfilment moments, director Harold Ramis forgot to give us anyone likeable to root for; even Wilson seems a bit charmless. Those in search of a superhero rom-com should stick to *Wonder Woman*.

DARKMAN

This Sam Raimi original is as much a tribute to the Universal horror icons of the 1930s as he is to superheroes like The Shadow or Batman, but he's still an unforgettable figure. Liam Neeson stars as Peyton Westlake, the scientific genius horribly disfigured by gangster Durant (Larry Drake) who seeks vengeance against his tormentor. The tragedy is that Westlake could go back to his own life, and that his girlfriend Julie (Frances McDormand) would accept him, but his own nature has changed, his anger has grown uncontrollable and he needs a crusade to keep his own wilder nature in check. Now that's dark, man.

UNBREAKABLE, SPLIT AND GLASS

It wasn't initially obvious that M. Night Shyamalan's 2000 hit *Unbreakable* was a superhero film; just that Bruce Willis's David Dunn had an uncanny knack for survival. And 2016's *Split*, starring James McAvoy as a multiple-personality serial killer, seemed to share only a director with that earlier film. Yet the two were linked, leading to 2019's crossover film *Glass*. Together, they offer a bold twist on superhero tropes, played in a sombre tone at a glacial pace. The first two films and first two thirds of the third film work brilliantly, until *Glass*'s final act fumbles the landing. But superhero films don't come any more idiosyncratic and original than this unusual trilogy.

MAN OF STEEL

AS CHRISTOPHER NOLAN COMPLETED HIS *DARK KNIGHT* TRILOGY, WARNER
BROS RETURNED TO THE THORNY QUESTION OF SUPERMAN. ONCE A JEWEL
IN THE STUDIO'S CROWN, HE'D LAIN DORMANT FOR YEARS. THE 2006 FILM
SUPERMAN RETURNS HAD FAILED, TOO INTROSPECTIVE IN NATURE TO RESTORE THE
SUPERHERO'S FORMER GLORY.

But screenwriter David S. Goyer and Nolan came up with a concept that they thought could work: a sort of "Superman Begins" approach that would re-establish Clark Kent and his alter-ego for a new generation. With *300* director Zack Snyder aboard to lead it, the result was a visually stunning Superman film that took the character in some unexpected directions.

We began on a reimagined Krypton – not the sterile and crystalline planet of the Christopher Reeve films,

but an ecosystem full of extraordinary things. It's a world where Russell Crowe's Jor-El can commute to work by dragon-thing and no one blinks an eyelid. But it's built on strict eugenics and genetic control;

Opposite Henry Cavill as Superman, in a redesigned costume that did away with the red knickers.

Below Laurence Fishburne as Daily Planet editor Perry White, with Amy Adams as Lois Lane.

Jor's son, Kal-El, is the first naturally born baby in a millennium. This is no tragic society, destroyed only by over-confidence, but a metaphor for our own energy hunger and environmental recklessness.

It's a wildly promising opening with all the scale and grandeur that one could wish for. But then we get into the younger years of a Kal-El/Clark Kent, who is less recognizable. Casting-wise, there's not much to quibble with. Henry Cavill looks like Superman, all idealized features and seraphic glow. Kevin Costner, with the weight of his all-American career behind him, makes a perfect Jonathan Kent, and Diane Lane is a younger and likeable Martha. But the idea that Jonathan orders the young Clark not to save his life, rather than risk provoking questions about his powers, feels like a stretch – way to give your son a complex, Mr Kent – and way to lose the comics' message that there are some things that even Superman can't prevent, such as age and a heart attack.

The film, however, cares less about what Superman *can't* do and more about what he can. It

Above Michael Shannon's General Zod is maniacally focused on resurrecting Krypton.

Opposite Russell Crowe is Jor-El, the doomed Kryptonian leader who foresees the coming disaster.

asks what it means to be Superman; to have almost godlike powers on a more-or-less realistic Earth. There's Jesus imagery – check out the moment when Superman floats out of a spaceship, arms outstretched, or his willingness to sacrifice himself to Michael Shannon's General Zod to protect the planet – but it goes beyond that into the film's very DNA. It's a fair question to wonder how humanity would react to this super-powered being. The problem is that Snyder also shows a Clark who is deeply ambivalent about his own abilities and uncertain about his role in the world. This alien doesn't seem entirely certain how Earth *should* react to him; there's no real conflict because he doesn't have a strong sense of his own

mission and so the psychology of the entire film feels a little murky. His adoptive father stressed secrecy to the extent that he lived a nomadic life, the better to hide his exploits. But his birth father tells him he's meant for more; that he has a destiny – and he accepts that, but tentatively.

The arrival of his father's old enemy (and murderer), Zod, on a mission to Krypton-form Earth, forces Clark to truly embrace the Superman mantle. But even at that point he is hesitant, pushed into each new action by necessity, rather than idealism. His final battle with Zod is an orgy of destruction that levels much of Metropolis in a way that is positively shocking for those raised on the Christopher Reeve Superman. There's little sense, in either his earlier Smallville battle against the Kryptonian warriors or in this final fight, that he makes a serious effort to mitigate the devastation or shift the battleground away from populated areas. It's really only in the final moments of their fight that Zod forces Superman to actively save lives, by directly and specifically

threatening a small family group. Up to that point, we've seen very little evidence of Superman, as opposed to the nomadic Clark, saving anyone – and that feels like a serious omission.

Still, strong casting helps to keep this film on the rails. Amy Adams makes a determined and tenacious Lois Lane; Laurence Fishburne is underused but utterly convincing as Perry White, and Shannon is superb as Zod, still trying to fulfil his inborn mission to protect Krypton long after the planet's destruction. Even smaller roles, like Richard Schiff as Dr Hamilton (the man who actually saves Metropolis before Superman gets back to the fight), are filled by gifted actors.

Happily, Snyder's superb eye means that the film looks gorgeous. Superman's suit may be duller than before, but that first leap for the clouds still shines, and his CG-assisted cloak gives him the air of a Baroque saint, floating in mid-air just above the outstretched hands of the world. Maybe in the end, this does reach a Superman we can believe in.

BIG HERO 6

DISNEY BOUGHT MARVEL IN 2009, CEMENTING THE CORPORATION'S HOLD ON EVERY PROPERTY WE LOVED IN OUR CHILDHOOD. THE MAIN MCU HAS BENEFITED HUGELY FROM HAVING THAT SINGLE STUDIO HOME, BUT IT'S A MISTAKE TO THINK THAT THAT WAS THE ONLY OUTCOME. THE DEAL ALSO OPENED UP OTHER, MORE OBSCURE MARVEL TITLES FOR ADAPTATION IN OTHER MEDIA, AND DISNEY ANIMATION'S TAKE ON *BIG HERO 6* WAS THE FIRST BIG-SCREEN RESULT.

The comic series, however, provide little beyond names and a few basic character traits to the finished film. Hiro Takachiho remains a teenage genius connected with a robot called Baymax, but onscreen, he gets a new surname and that robot a different origin story and original purpose: nurse, not bodyguard. Many of his team retain their names (Go-Go, Wasabi, Honey Lemon and Fred) but they lose original leader, the Silver Samurai, already onscreen in *The Wolverine*. Essentially, directors Don Hall and Chris Williams took a few concepts and ran in the other direction.

Their story is set in the gorgeous city of San Fransokyo: a sort of cross between the West-coast

Opposite Scott Adsit voices "personal healthcare companion" Baymax.

Below Hiro (Ryan Potter) and the titular sextet.

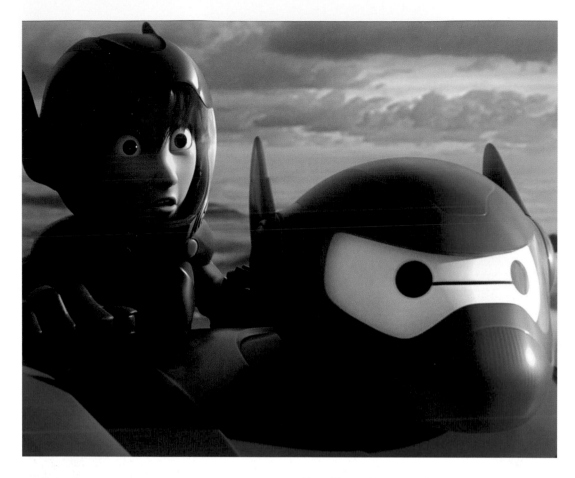

melting pot of San Francisco and the high-tech, neon-drenched streets of Tokyo. Hiro (voiced by Ryan Potter) becomes the focus of the team, though he starts as a teen tech genius squandering his gift on underground 'bot fights. His older brother, Tadashi (Daniel Henney), persuades him that he can do more, and motivates him to join him at the San Fransokyo Institute of Technology with Tadashi's mates, Go Go (Jamie Chung), Fred (T. J. Miller), Wasabi (Damon Wayans Jr) and Honey Lemon (Genesis Rodriguez).

Then disaster strikes. Tadashi is killed trying to save people in a fire, and Hiro is bereft – until he re-discovers Tadashi's final project: an inflatable nurse robot named Baymax (voiced by *30 Rock*'s Scott Adsit). This puffy, preternaturally calm creature just wants to do what's best for Hiro, and Hiro convinces him that he will be best assisted by finding out what

Above Hiro and a newly armoured Baymax fly around the city. You know, for health reasons.

Opposite Wasabi (Damon Wayans Jr) and Honey Lemon (Genesis Rodriguez) in action.

caused the fire that led to Tadashi's death – and that the quest will require a few militaristic alterations to Baymax's appearance and programming. "This armour may undermine my non-threatening, huggable design," worries the robot who was, after all, originally designed to look like a "walking marshmallow". And, "I fail to see how karate makes me a better healthcare companion" – but, in the end, it does.

Baymax is just a wonderful creation. From his first appearance, gingerly stepping from his charging case and carefully lifting aside a lab-stool to reach his patient, he's insanely likeable, like a giant balloon kitten. His delicacy of touch is gorgeous: watch him carefully apply small pieces of Sellotape to his own damaged arm, or picking his way around a crowded room to reach Hiro. The moment that he realizes Tadashi's absence is heartbreaking: he's relatively unevolved at that point and cannot, perhaps, understand the full implications of death, but even Baymax can sense that something monumental has gone wrong. And his concern for other characters is unfailing, but he can also show interest in the wider world and pursue a search for knowledge or beauty that is all his own: look at him chasing a butterfly in an unguarded moment.

The investigation into Tadashi's death uncovers a theft of Hiro's work and a threat to the whole city, one that will require all Six to band together to defeat. Which, of course, they do, though not in the way you might expect. But the group are tested along the way. Hiro is broken by his brother's death and obsessed

with the closure he believes he will have if he can solve it. For that to make sense, Tadashi has to make an indelible impression, in just a few scenes, as the best big brother ever: a protector, an inspiration, a partner in crime. And then Hiro has to commit a monstrous wrong before he realizes the error of his ways: he tries to make Baymax a killer, in a bone-deep betrayal of everything the robot, and Tadashi, stood for. It's only by realizing how far he's gone that Hiro reins himself in, earns his friends' trust once more and allows Baymax to do what he was designed to do: provide care to those in need.

In the end, of course, they beat the bad guy and save the world – though it's slightly more complicated than that, and the bad guy is also grieving. The win comes at a great and emotional cost to Hiro, but this time he's equipped to deal with it: he keeps his friends close, and that makes all the difference. It turns out that the key word in this title isn't "hero", it's the group of "six".

GUARDIANS OF THE GALAXY AND GUARDIANS OF THE GALAXY VOL. 2

PRIOR TO ABOUT 2012, THE GUARDIANS OF THE GALAXY WERE RELATIVELY OBSCURE, EVEN FOR MARVEL FANS, THEIR BOOK ONLY IN PRINT FOR A COUPLE OF YEARS FROM 2008 (FOLLOWING AN EARLIER RUN WITH A DIFFERENT LINE-UP IN THE LATE 1960s). BUT AMONG THEIR FANS WAS MARVEL BOSS KEVIN FEIGE, AND THAT MADE ALL THE DIFFERENCE.

He saw potential in their space capers, not least because that could make the MCU truly galactic in scope, and met with filmmaker James Gunn, to that point best known for gory, gonzo horror, to consider him for the job. It would prove a match made in heaven.

Gunn, it's fair to say, fell deeply in love with the characters. He reworked Nicole Perlman's script to fit his conception of the Guardians and crafted a story about an unlikely bunch of misfits who meet while squabbling over a bounty: an Orb in this case. They were all losers – which the film defines as "people who have lost something" – but by risking their lives together to save the galaxy, they not only redeem

Opposite ReePeter Quill / Starlord (Chris Pratt) in action on the first film's poster art.

Below The Guardians. Gamora (Zoe Saldana), Rocket (Bradley Cooper), Starlord, Groot (Vin Diesel) and Drax (Dave Bautista).

their past failures but also gain some measure of comfort for their griefs.

The whole thing depends on superb group dynamics, and Gunn created those with an excellent script and thanks to some surprising, even counter-intuitive casting. *Parks and Recreation*'s Andy Dwyer, aka actor Chris Pratt, didn't look like a matinee idol when he came in to audition. But Gunn knew he had the light comic chops and charisma he needed for the sometimes blustery Peter Quill/Starlord, so he cast him and trusted personal training to do the rest. Wrestler Dave Bautista was another risk, an almost untried actor who was quite literally sick with nerves at his audition. Only Zoe Saldana, as the tough, complicated Gamora, really made sense on paper, and luckily for Gunn, she agreed to be painted green. He then sprinkled a little star voice power on top in the form of Bradley Cooper as bio-engineered weapons nut Rocket and Vin Diesel as the "house plant-slash-muscle" Groot (Diesel came up with a surprising number of tonal variations on his one phrase "I am Groot").

But casting wasn't the only area where *Guardians...* swings for the fences. After that heartbreaking death-bed opening, we cut to an alien world, with an intrepid and rather cool explorer venturing deep into the ruins – before breaking into a dance to a 1970s classic. Clearly, this film is going to take the lived-in aesthetic of science fiction like *Star Wars* or *Alien* and inject it with a hefty dose of colour and funk. It's a little edgier than some other Marvel sub-franchises (that Jackson Pollock joke!) but the gags are so relentless and the characters so instantly iconic that it would take a hard heart to resist it. Just consider Rocket's "Oh. Yeah." as he opens fire during a prison break-out, or Groot's almost doggy grin after dismantling an entire battalion of enemy troops in a fit of vegetable fury.

Despite Gunn's lower-budget roots, he showed immediate and immense self-confidence: this story pauses for an eerie and beautiful light show by Groot in the middle of a battle, Marvel's most spectacular battle yet in terms of CG complexity (although admittedly, it was yet another example of a large flying thing threatening a major population

Above Rocket and Groot in action in poster art.

Below Karen Gillan as Nebula, a sometime villain who came to play a key role in Marvel's sprawling universe.

centre). His personality shapes those jokes and the anti-authoritarian attitude of the team, and if it also indulges in moments of frat-boy humour, Gamora's frown usually sets things back on track. At last the Guardians find it in themselves to come together and save the galaxy from Lee Pace's fanatical Ronan the Accuser, and despite the many ways they've denied being heroes, you buy it.

Of course, *Volume 2* sees them torn apart again, as Rocket unwisely tries to steal some super-batteries they've been hired to protect and incurs the wrath of an entire civilization. But the focus this time is even more on family. The entire team is protective of the young Baby Groot, who they're trying to raise to be a good tree/accomplice. Then Starlord meets his long-lost dad Ego, the Living Planet (Kurt Russell – and yes, superhero families are weird), and Gamora once again tangles with her psychotic cyborg sister, Nebula (Karen Gillen). The most developed and important relationship of the lot, perhaps

Above Michael Rooker's Yondu, Sean Gunn's Kraglin and the Ravagers, space-pirates who raised Quill.

surprisingly, is that between Quill and his adoptive father/former boss/current hunter, Yondu (Michael Rooker), who redeems a lifetime of thievery, piracy and general ne'er-doing-well with a glorious example of parenting ("That guy was a jackass," he sniffs of Ego) and a nod to *Mary Poppins*.

Even more than the first, this is a story about relationships, the families we're born with and the ones we choose for ourselves, the urge to push people away and why it's worth bringing them back. It says, in the end, that biological legacy is worthless if it isn't accompanied by love. But it also makes room for scenes of an impossibly cute baby tree running around a spaceship with a variety of prostheses and a severed toe. That kind of tonal tap-dancing is what keeps people coming back to this universe, and why James Gunn's band of misfits instantly gave Marvel a fillip.

ANT-MAN AND ANT-MAN AND THE WASP

IT'S IRONIC AND A LITTLE SAD THAT ANT-MAN BEGAN AS A PASSION-PROJECT FOR A MAN WHO DID NOT ULTIMATELY DIRECT THE FILM. EDGAR WRIGHT PITCHED KEVIN FEIGE AN ANT-MAN FILM BEFORE THE MCU EVEN EXISTED, WAY BACK IN 2004, AND REMAINED INVOLVED IN THE SCRIPT AND PRODUCTION FOR TEN YEARS BEFORE DEPARTING OVER CREATIVE DIFFERENCES.

His crusade to make the film, however, was not in vain: Ant-Man started as an also-ran, largely unpopular character, far from a priority for the new Universe, but became a key member of the superhero line-up and a contender for their most charming character.

Credit for the film must, therefore, be divided between Wright, who got a *long* way through casting and pre-production, and eventual director Peyton Reed. It matters that the casting is so on point. Paul

Rudd makes a likeably hangdog Scott Lang, someone who, OK, technically went to prison for robbery but was really always a crusader for the little guy. He's a little hapless, but not incompetent, and he loves his daughter, Cassie (Abby Ryder Fortson, who's super-charming and pleasantly weird). Sure, Lang loses

Opposite Paul Rudd as Scott Lang, the ex-con who becomes Ant-Man.

Below Ant-Man and his trusty ant-army race into battle.

Left Michael Peña's scene-stealing Luis with Tip "T.I." Harris' Dave and David Dastmalchian as Kurt, Scott's ex-con buddies.

Opposite In Ghost (Hannah John-Kamen), *Ant-Man and the Wasp* delivered one of the MCU's most sympathetic villains.

Below Evangeline Lily as Hope Van Dyne, soon to become the Wasp.

his first job after he's released, but that's because Baskin Robbins always finds out and not because he isn't trying.

As the original Ant-Man – the man who sets Lang up to take his place – Michael Douglas lent the film gravitas and a certain prickly sense of bossiness as Hank Pym. He invented the shrinking technology that powers all these suits and, boy, will he never let you forget it. Then there's Evangeline Lily as Hope, who absolutely convinces that she would make a far better Ant-Person than Scott, if only her father would get out of her way and allow her to put herself at risk. It would take a full film before she got her chance.

They're initially up against Corey Stoll's Darren Cross, a business executive and scientist who rediscovered Hank's old research and decided to market it for espionage and war (to create, as his marketing double-speak puts it, "a sustainable environment of well-being around the world." Ugh). It's a clash of attitudes as regards the dangerous tech: Hank's desire to keep it secret, keep it safe versus Darren's urge to market the hell out of it. There are echoes of the issues Tony Stark faces in the *Iron Man* films, and the film doesn't always justify Hank's belief that *this* tech is far more earth-shaking, but really it's all peripheral. This film is more concerned

with having fun than with reshaping the Marvel Universe; it's a throwback to 1980s action capers like *Inner Space* or *Honey, I Shrunk the Kids*.

And it really is fun. The pace is fast and furious, and the storytelling lightning-quick. That's mostly thanks to Michael Peña as Luis, Scott's irrepressibly cheery prison buddy, who regularly threatens to steal the show. This commendably cultured guy – as well

as his "mad thieving skills", he is into neo-Cubism, a bit of Rothko, a delightful *rosé* and the melancholy ballads of Morrisey – gets a bigger role in the sequel, but both films show that he should be Hollywood's officially-appointed narrator for everything.

That sequel, *Ant-Man and the Wasp*, works best when it essentially just plays with these characters. It's a film with a lot of empathy – for one of its villains, Hannah John-Kamen's Ghost, in particular, but even for ants eaten by seagulls – and loads more humour. It sometimes loses its sense of urgency, however: despite being under house arrest (after the events of Civil War) and being keen not to go back to prison, Scott does sometimes seem to get distracted by adventure instead of worrying about his future with his daughter. And despite Hope's Wasp being promoted to co-title character, she doesn't get much in the way of character development; we learn

essentially nothing about her that we didn't already know. But at least the film digs into the damage that losing the first Wasp, Janet (Michelle Pfeiffer), did to both Hope and Hank, and gives a path to recovery. It's the same for Ghost and Bill Foster (Laurence Fishburne): another (quasi) father-daughter pairing in need of help and small-h hope.

Again, any themes beyond the obvious family reunions more or less fade into the background behind the jokes ("You can do anything. You're the world's greatest grandma," Cassie encourages her dad). But the jokes are really good, and the characters are almost uniformly loveable. So perhaps it's enough simply to have a caper movie, without the entire world hanging on the outcome. If Scott needs higher stakes, he can hang out with the other Avengers, as in *Civil War* and *Endgame*. But his own films are lighter, and it's good just to have fun with superheroes sometimes.

THE CULT CLASSICS

THESE ARE THE FILMS THAT COULD, AND PERHAPS SHOULD, HAVE MADE THE MAIN LIST, BUT THEY'RE GATHERED HERE BECAUSE, WELL… THIS IS THE COOL-KIDS CLUB. MANY OF THESE FILMS DIDN'T MAKE A HUGE IMPACT AT THE BOX OFFICE, AND SOME EVEN FLOPPED. OTHERS ARE ONLY ARGUABLY SUPERHEROES, EITHER BECAUSE THEY LACK SUPER-POWERS OR HEROISM. STILL, THERE'S A LOT TO BE SAID FOR COMIC-BOOK MOVIES THAT TRY TO BREAK THE MOULD, OR ADOPT A SELF-CONSCIOUSLY UNIQUE STYLE. HERE ARE THE LOVEABLE MISFITS OF THE COMICS WORLD.

THE CROW (1994)

Best known, sadly, as the film on which star Brandon Lee tragically died in a stunt gone wrong, The Crow is now a testament to his strengths. Its story of a murder victim returned from the dead to hunt down his killers and those of his wife is pitch-black, but that none-more-Goth tone and dashes of ultra-violence made it stand out from the crowd.

TANK GIRL (1995)

Maybe the quintessential Riot Grrrl, Lori Petty makes a great heroine in a film that can't quite find its feet. At times it's highly cartoonish (there's no way to make her part-kangaroo boyfriend work, even if he is Ice-T) and at others it verges on *Mad Max*-level high stakes. Still, you have to love its attitude and that killer soundtrack.

DREDD (2012)

He's definitely based on a comic book, but would you call him a superhero? Perhaps it's safer to do so to his face, anyway. Karl Urban keeps the mask on as the Judge Dredd, jury and executioner of Mega City One, in a visually dazzling and gorgeously muscular story: fight all the bad guys, get to the drug kingpin (Lena Headey), try not to die.

THE ROCKETEER (1991)

This feels like a prototype for later super-films: the tech is a bit Iron Man-y, the setting is pure Captain America and Hulk's Jennifer Connelly is the love interest. But Joe "First Avenger" Johnston gives real heart to this Saturday-morning serial-style adventure, and ILM's effects add a sheen and scale to the derring-do.

MYSTERY MEN (1999)

A gang of wannabes with questionable powers steps into the breach when their city's real superhero (Greg Kinnear) is captured by bad guy Casanova Frankenstein (Geoffrey Rush). The cast is as good as that name – Ben Stiller, William H. Macy, Janeane Garolfo – and if the jokes are hit-and-miss, there are enough of them to keep you laughing. An underrated pleasure.

THE PHANTOM (1996)

Billy Zane is the latest in an ancient line of masked warriors in this fun, silly romp: think Indiana Jones in spandex. Technically, though, there are some powers involved in his skull ring, and it's certainly based on a classic comic, so it counts. This Simon Wincer adaptation (he also made *Free Willy*) is part of a mini-trend for 1990s films set in the comic-book Golden Age of the 1930s and 1940s.

THE SHADOW (1994)

Who knows what evil lurks in the hearts of men? This guy! Alec Baldwin stars as the mystically reformed crimefighter Shadow, who must stop a descendant of Genghis Khan from taking over the world. With *Highlander*'s Russell Mulcahy in charge, it's a stylish affair but one with some rather dodgy ethnic stereotypes and lots of mystical hokum.

KICK-ASS AND KICK-ASS 2 (2010/2013)

Adapted from Mark Millar and Jon Romita Jr's comic, Matthew Vaughn's film imagines a world where people fight crime without the benefit of powers or a huge amount of money. The results are bone-crackingly violent, extremely foul-mouthed and in terrible taste – so wildly entertaining. Jeff Wadlow's sequel is a little less successful, but still shocks

WANTED (2008)

Another deliberately bad-taste Mark Millar comic, this story of super-assassins who live entirely outside the law was cleaned up a bit before reaching the screen to make it palatable. Happily, they kept the curving bullets, high death toll and general disrespect for the laws of physics. James McAvoy's good, but Angelina Jolie has never been cooler.

SWAMP THING (1981)

Wes Craven took a break from pure horror for this likeable monster movie, wherein the classic comics character gets an origin story, a damsel in distress (Adrienne Barbeau) and a chance to chase paramilitary leader Arcane (Louis Jourdan) out of his marshy home. It's campy fun, but the suit is limited, even by the standards of its day.

BATMAN V SUPERMAN: DAWN OF JUSTICE

ZACK SNYDER'S ANNOUNCEMENT THAT THE SEQUEL TO *MAN OF STEEL* WOULD BE A BATMAN V SUPERMAN FILM WAS MADE IN HALL H AT SAN DIEGO COMIC-CON IN 2013, AT THE CLIMAX OF A WARNER BROS SLATE PRESENTATION THAT HAD INCLUDED JEFF BRIDGES AND TOM CRUISE AS WARM-UP ACTS.

One man near me in the audience practically re-enacted the diner scene from *When Harry Met Sally*, loudly yelling, "Yes! Yes! Yes!" in a breathless baritone. Something about the match-up – man vs god, as the film puts it – is a perennial fascination for fans, the ultimate "who would win in a fight". It was catnip to fans.

Now let's be real: Superman would win. Literally, in a heartbeat. You can natter on about Batman's strategic genius and access to Kryptonite and what's happened in the comics as much as you want, and yet it will still be true (not only because Superman is himself, canonically, at least a "Level 8 intelligence" and probably as high as 10). The only force that dictates that Batman could ever win is narrative tension, and logic demands a little more. So every time you play this scenario, you have to justify not only why these two heroes would fight, but also why Superman doesn't disable or kill Batman faster than the latter can even sense his presence. Snyder just about manages the former, at least in the Ultimate Edition cut, and impressively gives the Big Blue Boy Scout a reason to keep the Bat alive.

He also does a few bits of clever storytelling. If the worst decision in *Man of Steel* was that final orgy of destruction, the best decision of this sequel was to put Bruce Wayne at ground level of the scene to explain why he might object to the Kryptonian presence on Earth. There's a suggestion that both men are suffering from trauma after that fight; this is a Superman still

unsure of his role and uncertain if he's doing any good in life, and a Batman hardened by his unending fight.

Batman quotes Dick Cheney's one per cent doctrine, as nonsensical and paranoid a thought as has ever been formulated, and seems irrational in his dogged determination of Superman (the ultimate edition

Opposite Ben Affleck's Batman faces off against Henry Cavill's Superman.

Below Jeremy Irons steps in as Alfred Pennyworth, Batman's better half.

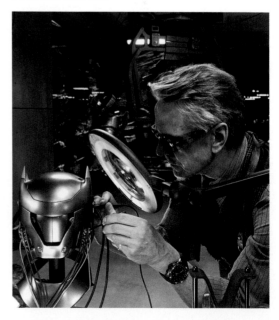

makes it clearer that those flames are being deliberately fanned, on both sides, by Jesse Eisenberg's Lex Luthor). Whatever Batman's one rule is, whether it's no guns or no killing, he smashes it here. The argument is that he's older, more cynical, that he's been worn down by his long crusade. But there are certain things that are non-negotiable, without which you don't have Batman, just a dude with a cool car. A Superman who doesn't make saving people his focus also feels unrecognizable; in the theatrical cut here, he leaves an exploded US Congress without visibly helping the wounded.

There are also a high number of visions for a film that is trying to inject reality into these characters' lives. Batman sees a future where DC uber-villain Darkseid rules (judging by that giant Omega sign carved into the desert) and Superman has gone bad; Superman has an entire conversation with his adoptive father's ghost. Never mind a time-travelling Flash (Ezra Miller) dropping in with an apparently apocalyptic warning to Bruce. Blame the endless chat about gods, and Snyder's not-quite-realized plan for a five-film arc across the *Justice League* films as well.

In the end, Batman and Superman sort out their differences – of course – and bond over their mothers' shared first name – eh? – and team up to take down Luthor and the Doomsday monster he has created. As

JUSTICE LEAGUE

It should have been the sort of victory-lap triumph that *Avengers* was, but somehow this team-up of the DC heroes never quite works. Wonder Woman remained charming; Aquaman and the Flash injected humour and charisma, and Bat-fleck was dryly witty, so it should have worked. But CG villain Steppenwolf looked like a goth cousin to Tim Curry's demon in *Legend* and acted like a bargain-basement Zod, while the fight scenes saw the entire League take bafflingly ill-conceived decisions. By the time Superman is resurrected to save the day, it's too late; it's a mish-mash of characters and tones that never quite gelled.

Above A heavily armoured Batman confronts his Kryptonian opponent.

Opposite Gal Gadot's Diana is introduced a mysterious presence at Lex Luthor's party.

comic-book lore dictates he must, Superman dies in the conflict against the beast, despite the help of a freshly introduced Wonder Woman (Gal Gadot), who comes with the film's best character theme and a fierce sense of joy in the fight. "Is she with you?" asks Superman – but of course, she is her own woman, and would outshine them both next time.

"The dead shall live" says the minister at Clark's funeral, and we sense that this one, at least, definitely will. The *Justice League* movie was already announced; we know that Steppenwolf is coming, and sure enough the earth atop the coffin moves, just slightly, so we know that the Earth will move for Lois again one day soon. Still, there's nobility in Snyder's attempt to make a psychological drama out of what could have been just another super-brawl. It's overly dour and lacking in tonal variation, but – at least in the ultimate edition – there's substance, and character development. Batman's opening monologue says there are no "diamond absolutes" and that "things fall". By the end, he has regained his faith, and the stage is set for a more recognizable, more heroic Batman (and perhaps Superman) in the future. Or so it seemed.

DEADPOOL AND DEADPOOL 2

FOR YEARS, THE PROSPECT OF A DEADPOOL FILM HUNG AROUND HOLLYWOOD LIKE THE SMELL OF FRESH BREAD PUMPED OUT OF AN EMPTY BAKERY, TANTALIZING FANS AND STUDIO EXECUTIVES BUT WITH NOTHING TO SHOW FOR IT.

After all, the "Merc with the Mouth" was a super-violent comedian who makes light of the carnage he causes; a Looney-Tunes Wolverine aware of his own artificial nature. How do you explain that to an audience that considers *Hellboy* a bit out there?

Ryan Reynolds was first attached to star as Deadpool in 2004; eventual director Tim Miller in 2010 – and yet it still took until 2016 to reach cinemas. There were missteps along the way – that *X-Men Origins: Wolverine* version that died on the vine, or Reynolds' *Green Lantern*, which threatened to scupper his chance. But when Miller, Reynolds and the team finally convinced 20th Century Fox to take a risk on a filthy-minded, R-rated superhero satire, the result would prove a mega-hit, and the black sheep of the X-Men family would become one of its shining lights.

Let's be honest: Deadpool would be *exhausting* to be around. The relentless quippery and frivolity would get old quickly, as would his ability to recover from any injury short of... well, it's not clear what it would take to actually kill him. But onscreen, he is a whole lot of fun, from those ridiculous opening credits ("Produced by Asshats. Written by The Real Heroes Here") to the endless pop-culture references – most of them clever enough to have remained funny a few years on. It's lovely to see a man who is sufficiently secure in his masculinity to admit to his love of divas from Salt 'n' Pepa to Enya to Celine Dion; the latter even recorded the second film's Bond-esque title song.

That's one of the marked differences between the two *Deadpool* films: that second outing, on the back

of a hit, has a budget. The first one keeps things – in superhero terms – relatively reined in, with most of its time sustained by Reynolds riffs, rather than CG spectacle. It also allows space for an effective love story; there's real heat between Wade and Morena Baccarin's Vanessa, two wary and damaged people who fit together perfectly. And, er, repeatedly. But given that flippancy is a way of life for Wade, he needs someone like Vanessa, who's expert in the same thing, to see through to the pain and fury underneath.

That said, there's slaughter galore too: that opening freeway chase/fight ends with a score of bad guys shot, beheaded, branded and/or crushed, even if it does so to Juice Newton's version of "Angel of the Morning", a Reynolds suggestion for its profound

Above Wade and his true love Vanessa (Morena Baccarin) face his cancer diagnosis.

Opposite Deadpool / Wade Wilson (Ryan Reynolds) getting high on his own supply.

contrast to the scene's visuals. Wade Wilson may look "like I got bit by a radioactive Shar-pei" but he's a remarkably effective killer.

In the comics, Deadpool has often been paired with Spider-Man, because his flippancy contrasts rather well with Peter Parker's goodness. The comics go further, pairing him with solid straight man Colossus to contrast to Deadpool's unrestrained id. For the sequel, comics favourite Cable (Josh Brolin), a time-travelling warrior of unsurpassed seriousness, fulfils the same function. But *Deadpool 2* had the difficult task of recapturing lightning in a bottle, and it wasn't initially clear that David Leitch would manage it. The first act isn't promising: Vanessa is tragically killed off, even though the dead girlfriend is the most tired trope in Hollywood (see almost every Christopher Nolan film for further examples). It may have put 'pool in a deadlier, more desperate headspace, but there are less hackneyed ways of leaving him isolated.

The threat posed by Cable to tormented orphan Russell (Julian Dennison, essentially reprising his *Hunt for the Wilderpeople* role, which is not a criticism) should have been enough to send even an anti-hero into action without the prior trauma. It all means that the film flounders in unnatural solemnity until Deadpool realizes he needs back-up to stop Cable and recruits a team he calls "X-Force". This assassin is a social animal as loners go and he bounces beautifully off Zazie Beetz's Domino, Rob Delaney's Peter, and the rest. Then we can enjoy the antics as our anti-hero gets horribly injured and grotesquely mutilated, and when he leads his team into disaster.

Above, left Josh Brolin as time-traveller Cable.

Above Domino (Zazie Beetz), a mutant with the power of luck.

Opposite Deadpool recreates Flashdance with more bullet casings.

The sequel is a bigger film that hews a little more closely to superhero tropes than its predecessor (one of the mid-credit stings here actually matters, unlike the first film's post-credit Ferris Bueller homage) and replays a few jokes (if you were grossed out by Deadpool growing a new hand from scratch, wait until he regrows his entire lower half!). But for the Juggernaut's choral theme alone, *Deadpool 2* would earn its place – and it gets bonus points for the ridiculous "Once Upon a Deadpool" PG re-release, wherein our hero kidnaps *The Princess Bride*'s Fred Savage and forces him to listen to a censored version of the entire film as a bedtime story. That slight blemish on his record aside, Deadpool may dismiss superheroes as "lame-ass teachers' pets" but he ends up earning a place among them. Or at least one standing right behind, making sarky comments and rude gestures while they're not paying attention.

DOCTOR STRANGE

IF *THOR* INTRODUCED THE CONCEPT OF ALIEN CIVILIZATIONS TO THE MCU AND *GUARDIANS OF THE GALAXY* TOOK US SOARING OUT AROUND THE COSMOS, *DOCTOR STRANGE* OPENS THAT SHARED UNIVERSE TO ENTIRELY NEW DIMENSIONS OF REALITY IN ANOTHER QUANTUM LEAP FORWARD.

Strange was created by Steve Ditko, one of the comic-book visionaries of Marvel's Silver Age, and it was a title where he let his imagination run wild with trippy, colourful results. Those stories are a world away from the straightforward heroism of the other Avengers – full of metaphysical problems, clashes with the supernatural and timey-wimey stuff.

Strange has been mooted for film development since the 1980s; Wes Craven and Guillermo del Toro were among those who tried to make it. But Kevin Feige and Marvel established the rest of their universe first, as a sort of baseline reality, and only then did they get mystical. Similarly, director Scott Derrickson eases us in gently. We open with the theft of certain pages from a temple library filled with old books to establish some sort of threat, but quickly we cut to Benedict Cumberbatch's arrogant surgeon, Stephen Strange. He's rich, entitled and has a put-upon girlfriend in Rachel McAdams' underserved Christine.

When a car accident ends his career, however, he finds himself desperate for answers and travelling to Kathmandu, seeking the temple of Kamar-Taj and the Ancient One (Tilda Swinton) who might be able to cure him. But instead of simply fixing his hands, she opens his eyes. He learns of – and slowly, reluctantly, becomes involved with – a great war between levels of reality and, particularly, against a monster outside time called Dormammu.

It's extreme, but not unrelatable. Who among us has not had the urge to fall at Tilda Swinton's feet

and shakily beg, "Teach me"? What scientist and autodidact wouldn't grasp at infinite dimensions of new knowledge that go beyond the accepted limits of space and time? Who wouldn't want to study alongside Chiwetel Ejiofor's Mordo and, ideally, end up more like him? If anyone is slinging magic around New York City, you absolutely believe that these guys would be at the root of it.

We might not master a vast library of magical know-how in approximately six months, as Strange canonically does (an improbably short space of time, even by the standard of these movies), but we'd still try. Really, the plot – requiring Strange, Mordo, Benedict Wong's Wong and the Ancient One to stop Mads Mikkelsen's Kaecilius from going full dark side and bringing Dormammu to destroy the Earth – is less important than the fact of that education.

The task is for him to overcome his fear of failure, the flaw that led him to turn down too-difficult surgical cases in favour of the tricky-but-fixable ones that would maintain his perfect record. As the Sorcerer Supreme he becomes, he has to learn to let go of the things he cannot control, but also to take on the challenges that seem impossible. It's a lesson he learns well: his victory against Dormammu is the result of failing thousands of times first, and he would learn to

Opposite Benedict Cumberbatch stars as the well-named Dr Stephen Strange, surgeon turned sorcerer supreme.

fail again in *Infinity War*. But then, as the Ancient One tells him, "It's not about you." It's about giving up his own hunt for glory in order to achieve greatness.

First, of course, he must defeat Kaecilius, using the Time Stone to undo his destruction of Hong Kong and fighting the apostate through a city where time is otherwise flowing backward and buildings are repairing themselves. In scenes like this, *Doctor Strange* looks unlike any film you've ever seen. Reality is splintered into fractals like glass by these sorcerers, almost at a whim. People travel through portals in sparking Catherine Wheels and draw mandalas in fire in mid-air. Walls and solid surfaces are folded, magnified and turned into spinning gears, as if the

world itself becomes clockwork. Perhaps that's appropriate given that these people are charged with holding and protecting the Time Stone. However you twist it, this takes the sort of effects pioneered in Christopher Nolan's *Inception* and twists them further in Escher-like landscapes that challenge the eye's ability to keep track.

Still, confusion is as it should be for the Sorcerer Supreme; our tiny mortal minds are not meant to ken all the things that he comprehends. A little madness, a little mystery and even a little mysticism seem proper. We can only dream of following him outside the bounds of time, physics and reality itself, into a world where truly anything is possible.

Opposite, above The Ancient One (Tilda Swinton) punches Strange onto the astral plane.

Above Karl Mordo (Chiwetel Ejiofor) is a potent ally of Strange, until their aims begin to drift apart.

Left Strange and Mordo face the twisting landscape of New York as they stand in the Mirror Dimension.

SUICIDE SQUAD

IT'S A SOLID IDEA: SEND IN THE BAD GUYS – THE EXPENDABLES IF YOU WILL – TO THE SITUATIONS TOO MESSY FOR SUPERHEROES. THESE ANTI-HEROES AND OUTRIGHT VILLAINS BECOME THE SUICIDE SQUAD, A COLOURFUL AND CHARISMATIC BUNCH OF WEIRDOS – PARTICULARLY MARGOT ROBBIE'S HARLEY QUINN AND WILL SMITH'S DEADSHOT.

But while this was an interesting departure for gritty drama director David Ayers and a bigger hit than *Justice League* (to everyone's surprise), it's also an oddly scrappy film.

We start slow. There's a prison tour of Harley Quinn and Deadshot's cells with some chat about their abilities, a lecture from agent Waller (Viola Davis) on everyone's histories and arrests, and a tooling-up scene with banter that sheds more light on the gang. It's an inefficient set-up, but it eventually communicates that these people have done Bad Things with their extraordinary abilities. At least by the time they land in a crisis in Midway City, however, we have a basic grasp on who's whom – even if we're still not clear what's keeping Flash or Batman away.

Above Margot Robbie's Harley Quinn proved to be a highlight of the ensemble cast.

Opposite A publicity shot from the film showing the entire Suicide Squad, who are never this close in real life.

The team is led by Joel Kinneman's straight-laced Rick Flag, Waller's proxy. Then there's Deadshot, lethal even with a potato gun, who allowed himself to be brought in by Batman, rather than disappoint his daughter. Harley's a gorgeous, flirtatious psycho longing to be reunited with her deeply abusive boyfriend, the Joker (Jared Leto). Jai Courtenay gets his best role in years as Captain Boomerang, a giggling lunatic with a better sense of self-preservation than the rest, and you may have sympathy for Diablo, Jay Hernandez's reformed gang member. They're up against a woman who was supposed to be one of their own, Enchantress: an ancient goddess in the body of archaeologist June Moone (Cara Delevingne). Alas, she may be a supermodel, but she doesn't make the greatest supervillain.

Ayers has the courage of his convictions, starting the deaths early (so long Adam Beach's Slipknot, we hardly knew ya) and keeping them mounting. But it takes more than a bit of the old ultra-violence. The idea is that the gang are forced to reckon with their pasts and what they want from the future as they fight their way through an occupied city to stop Enchantress, but there's relatively little sense of growth for most of them, because the film wants to keep emphasizing how bad they are, guys. At least a quick stop for a drink at the

Opposite Harley Quinn (Margot Robbie), Killer Croc (Adewale Akinnuoye-Agbaje), Katana (Karen Fukuhara), Rick Flag (Joel Kinnaman), Deadshot and Boomerang (Jai Courtney)

Below Enchantress (Cara Delevingne) threatens a city and perhaps, tomorrow, the world.

third-act turn allows for some proper bonding, and a marginally more heroic decision to actively participate in the job they were originally forced to undertake.

The final battle is a defeat-the-CG-baddie brawl, but it offers little moments of heroism for Deadshot, Harley and Diablo. Then they're all sent back to prison, albeit this time with a few perks: an espresso maker for Harley (like she needs the caffeine) and a visit with his daughter for Deadshot.

It's all slightly less satisfying than it should be. Smith and Ayers can't seem to agree on just how much of a scumbag Deadshot should be, so his characterization slips around. Leto's Joker is a demented, squeaky-voiced gangster without obvious redeeming feature, so that it becomes hard to tell why Dr Quinzel would find him hypnotic. The film also uses its "they're-bad-guys" excuse to indulge in a miserable level of misogyny, with Slipknot punching a woman almost as soon as we meet him and good-ish guy Deadshot telling Flag that he should smack Enchantress. The characterization – or lack thereof – of Katana doesn't help, while the truly formidable Harley is crippled by her romantic obsession.

Still, the appetite at the box office (over $740 million worldwide) despite poor reviews shows that there is an appetite for super-people behaving badly onscreen; *Venom* would suggest the same. Still, it's hard to make a mainstream film about entirely bad people. If there are no shades of grey, no points of light, there's just as much danger of tedium from bad guys as bland, 2D heroes. So maybe it's best, in the end, that the Suicide Squad offer enough decency to give us a little hope for their future.

WONDER WOMAN

HOLLYWOOD'S LINE FOR DECADES WAS THAT FEMALE-LED SUPERHERO FILMS DON'T WORK. *SUPERGIRL*, *CATWOMAN*, *ELEKTRA*: NONE OF THEM SET THE WORLD ALIGHT. BUT WHAT THAT CONVENTIONAL WISDOM FAILED TO TAKE INTO ACCOUNT IS THAT THOSE FILMS ARE ALL PRETTY BAD. IT'S LIKE WATCHING *GREEN LANTERN*, *BATMAN AND ROBIN* AND *SPAWN* AND CONCLUDING THAT MEN CAN'T MAKE GREAT LEADS.

The secret, as it turned out, was simple. They just needed to make a female-led superhero film that was halfway decent; a film that worried less about winning over male fans and more about giving girls a role model of their own.

The first key decision was hiring director Patty Jenkins to bring Diana of Themyscira – or Wonder Woman, as we call her – to the screen. Jenkins sought to create the hero that she would have wanted as a little girl, not some cheap girl-power pin-up. This Diana is still gorgeous – heart-stoppingly so, thanks to Gal Gadot – but she's also naïve, confused, determined, selfless, tough, idealistic and endlessly compassionate. In the hands of Jenkins and Gadot, Diana captures the contradictory nature of the Amazons, the warriors created to end war, but she is far beyond them in power and potential – as she gradually learns.

The first key to getting *Wonder Woman* right was creating Themyscira itself, the paradise island where she grows up, the only child among a race of powerful women. It seemed a little hokey in the old Lynda Carter-starring TV series, but here it's a stunning reversal of the usual film ratios. Most of the time onscreen, we see a population that is 70 per cent male; it is radical to show a world that is 100 per cent female,

and filled with physically strong, highly opinionated, deeply authoritative women. This is the world that shaped Princess Diana; a world where peace is not only possible but normal. It's also a world lacking in prejudice or sexism, a sharp contrast to her experience of wartime London and its strict gender roles and ridiculous clothing. Diana has much to set right.

So the pivotal scene where Wonder Woman, still newly arrived in man's world, steps up from a World War I trench is enough to send chills down your spine. She is a woman stepping into the most dangerous environment on Earth, a place where nothing can survive: No Man's Land in more ways than one. And then she begins to flick bullets away with a slash of her wrist, to bat aside mortars and speed from a walk to a run across the wasteland. Her actions create a hole in the German defences into which the Allies follow her, but that's not what the scene is about: it's a repudiation of the whole horrific business of modern war and an assumption of responsibility for peace. Diana always wanted to be a warrior, and was trained to fight; she has no compunction in killing if that will save lives in the end. But the devastating

Opposite Wonder Woman prepares to strike a blow for female superheroes.

total war of World War I is anathema to her; it is the sort of injustice she was born to oppose.

That single scene warrants the shift of Wonder Woman's World War II comic-book origin to the earlier conflict. We can all agree that Nazis are bad, but there's no such moral clarity in World War I; it was a grotesque waste of lives that should never have happened, spurred on by arrogant old men on both sides. Where better to introduce an Amazon superhero to the mix? It takes a while for Diana to realize that the two sides are almost equally compromised, but her heartbreak when she does echoes the way that entire generations were disillusioned by that conflict.

That clash between cynicism and idealism also colours her relationship with Chris Pine's Steve Trevor. As a spy, he's fascinated by her honesty, swept away by her beauty, thrown off his game just by the sight of her. He teaches her about the world, sure, but it's not a patronizing know-all educating the little lady; it's an exchange. She gains his knowledge and, in return, he gets some of his eroded idealism back, even in the worst moments of the war. He gains

Above Diana with her mother, Queen Hippolyta (Connie Nielsen), in the throne room of Themyscira.

Opposite, above Diana and her World War I squad: Sameer (Saïd Taghmaoui), Steve Trevor (Chris Pine), Chief Napi (Eugene Brave Rock) and Charlie (Ewen Bremmer).

Opposite, below Diana proves that No Man's Land poses no danger for a Wonder Woman.

as much, or more, as she does. She also seems to heal all those who spend time with her, giving some sort of comfort to Steve's motley cohorts.

Not everything works so well: the final, heavily CG conflict against the war god, Ares, is heavy on the CG punching and lighter than it should be on emotion. Still, Jenkins keeps the ship steady and the themes clearly in sight. In the end, like Steve Rogers before him, Steve Trevor must crash a plane to save thousands of lives. Diana's overwhelming, explosive grief takes her powers to another level; it's not hatred that enables her to defeat Ares but the extent of her love. Nothing could be more appropriate to this hero. "I'm the man who can!" says Diana, emphatically. She's not wrong.

SUPER-DUDS
THE SUPERHERO FILMS YOU'D RATHER FORGET

NOT EVERY SUPER-FILM SPAWNS A FRANCHISE OR EVEN A SUCCESSFUL LINE OF TOYS. SOME SINK AT THE BOX OFFICE WITH BARELY A RIPPLE. THEY'RE REMEMBERED AS A PUNCHLINE OR AN EXAMPLE OF WHAT NOT TO DO. IT'S USUALLY NOT THE ACTOR'S FAULT (EXCEPT MAYBE IN ONE CASE BELOW) BUT IT'S QUITE OFTEN DOWN TO NEGLECTING THE THING THAT MAKES A CHARACTER WORK ON THE PAGE. AND WEIRDLY, THE EXAMPLES BELOW SUGGEST THAT MESSING UP THE LOOK OF A CHARACTER CAN BE FATAL. SO THESE ARE STORIES OF DUDS IN MORE THAN ONE SENSE.

CATWOMAN

It looked so good on paper: "Halle Berry" and "Catwoman" is a pretty sexy prospect whatever your orientation. But something about the plot – which sees Catwoman facing Sharon Stone's evil cosmetics tycoon with unbreakable skin thanks to her super-skincare regime (really) – felt patronizing and naff. Worse was that hellish costume of bootcut leather trousers, strategically ripped, and a couple of belts with aspirations as her top. French director Pitof hasn't made a big-screen movie since, and Berry retired gratefully back to playing Storm.

JUDGE DREDD

There's one rule if you're going to play *2000AD*'s fascist lawman. You. Never. Take. Off. The. Helmet. But what big studio pays for Sylvester Stallone and doesn't show his face? Far worse was the film's muddled tone. Director Danny Cannon, who's gone on to huge TV success, wanted a dark, bloody satirical film in line with the comics. Stallone planned a funny, comic PG-13 blockbuster. The result took five attempts to tone down the violence enough to get an R-rating and pleased almost no one.

ELEKTRA

In *Daredevil*, Jennifer Garner's Elektra had enough chemistry with Ben Affleck's Matt Murdock to shine, but she's cast adrift in this spin-off. Working as an assassin and assigned to kill Goran Visnjic's Mark Miller and his daughter, she tries to save them instead. The effects and, importantly, fights are OK, but the tone is so unrelentingly heavy that it weighs the whole film down. You have to wonder, too, why Elektra fights to save anyone when resurrection is apparently an easy and quick process.

SPAWN

Some will argue that this is a cult classic. They are, respectfully, wrong. Credit where it's due, Michael Jai White's Spawn was the first serious black superhero to break through on the big screen, and that's quite a lot, given how few have followed him. But the film's poor effects distract from White's efforts, and John Leguizamo's The Violator is, perhaps, the most irritating bad guy ever.

STEEL

The basic idea of casting Shaquille O'Neal as a sort of blue-collar Batman is a pretty good one, and casting Annabeth Gish as his wheelchair-user tech guru verges on great. Alas, while O'Neal *looks* like the kind of superhero who could take down dastardly arms dealer Judd Nelson, he moves like a mammoth and is perhaps not cinema history's greatest actor. There's a really likeable idea here, but disappointing execution.

THE SPIRIT

Based on the classic Will Eisner strip but failing to do it justice, this Frank Miller-written and -directed film looks pretty cool but never connects on a story or character level. The overtly noir, designed-to-death style had been done before – notably in Miller's own *Sin City* and Warren Beatty's *Dick Tracy* (neither included here, as they are not superhero films) – but you need more than that to make a compelling film. A sad waste of a great cast, given the presence of people like Samuel L. Jackson, Sarah Paulson, Eva Mendes and Scarlett Johansson.

GREEN LANTERN

A mess of CG suits and bizarre design decisions made this a trial to watch, and somehow much of this superhero-origin story felt tired and played-out, even relatively early in the superhero boom years. Happily, no one has dunked on the disappointing results harder than star Ryan Reynolds himself. In *Deadpool 2*, his Merc with the Mouth actually shot his younger self in the head, rather than allow him to take the role. It would have been a mercy really.

HOWARD THE DUCK

It's a George Lucas-produced superhero movie featuring Lea Thompson and Tim Robbins: what could go wrong? Well, he's an alien duck with a human girlfriend so rest assured that very little goes right. The prosthetics are beautifully designed but, y'know, human-sized duck suits just aren't capable of much expression. This one goes down in the history books as the very first theatrically released Marvel movie, but otherwise it's best left alone.

FANTASTIC FOUR

A cast composed almost entirely of gifted young actors do their best, but Josh Trank's darker take on the subject is all smell and no coffee. Most of the running time is spent with the quartet growing up, arguing, and then being locked up in separate cells once they have gained their powers. Their origin is reimagined as drunken male bonding, so that Kate Mara's Sue Storm doesn't even get to be involved, and Doom is barely introduced before it's time to wrap up. A real shame.

Contrary to popular opinion, lead actress Helen Slater is not the problem with *Supergirl*. She's just as upright and honest as her "cousin", Christopher Reeve's Superman, though she lacks an alter-ego as charming as Clark Kent. The problem is the film's hokey, too-broad tone, undermining every effort by Slater and her mentor, Zaltar (Peter O'Toole), to give it weight. The effects look cheap – though not much worse than the latter *Superman* films – and aside from giving "Linda Lee" a silly schoolgirl crush, the filmmakers seem not to consider how a female-led super-story might differ from a male one.

THE LEAGUE OF
EXTRAORDINARY GENTLEMEN

It all looked so good on paper: an Alan Moore graphic novel, based on classic characters from nineteenth-century literature, with Sean Connery leading the cast of the film adaptation. But director Stephen Norrington couldn't quite bring everything together. Too much of the film's budget went on Connery, and too little on surrounding him with stars of a similar calibre, which might have been fine had the script offered fully rounded characters and sensible plotting. The reviews were horrible; sadly, because this stands as Connery's final film

LOGAN

WHEN HUGH JACKMAN AND JAMES MANGOLD FIRST STARTED KICKING AROUND IDEAS FOR A THIRD STAND-ALONE WOLVERINE FILM, THEY QUICKLY AGREED ON ONE THING: IT SHOULD OFFER AN ENDING FOR THE CHARACTER AS WELL AS THE ACTOR, WHO WANTED TO GO OUT ON A HIGH.

It should be R-rated and uncompromising – not simply so that they could go to town on the violence, but so they could fold in more adult themes and be free of the budgetary obligation to go bigger and broader. They would, in fact, be limited in budget and forced to rely on character scenes instead of action dazzle. And it should take everything best about comics like Old Man Logan, but be beholden to none of them. The result was a triumph, easily the best

Wolverine film and arguably the most mature comic-book-superhero film ever made.

To start, Mangold sat down and tried to figure out what would truly scare his metal-boned hero. The

Opposite This is the story of a grizzled, older Logan (Hugh Jackman), but at least he's getting out into nature.

Below Logan with Laura (Dafne Keene), the girl he reluctantly transports across a hostile US.

answer he came up with was, perhaps, a surprising one: love. It would take a connection, a relationship, to really unsettle him and make him vulnerable. Wolverine himself can always heal; it's those around him who bear the brunt of violence and get lost along the way. Next to that, what's a Sabretooth more or less?

Jackman enthusiastically agreed, and worked hand-in-glove with Mangold to reinvent Logan in a way that's not *entirely* contradictory to what's gone before but which could equally take place in a parallel universe (many viewers prefer that interpretation, otherwise this undermines the "happy mansion" coda to *X-Men: Days of Future Past*). This Logan is beaten-up, older, and his healing factor is beginning to fail against the toxic adamantium on his bones.

The opening fight scene, against a gang of toughs trying to steal his car, results in something very close to defeat; Logan is no longer a one-man army but a fading tough guy trying to nurse a sick old man, Patrick Stewart's ailing Charles Xavier.

Then he's saddled with a little girl named Laura (Dafne Keen), an apparently mute mutant who has been communicating with Charles mentally. She gives Charles hope for the future – hope that their species isn't dead – and with her claws and ferocious fighting style, she might be a clone or the engineered offspring of Logan himself. But he considers her another complication he doesn't need, and cares only about keeping Charles safe (witness the scene in the farmhouse where he ignores Laura's plight to run after Charles).

The trio end up on the run across country, trying to find a possibly mythical place of safety that Laura believes is waiting. This is where the comparisons to Westerns really kick in, in the vast, sun-soaked landscapes and their encounters with, for example, the hard-working farm family of Eriq La Salle's

Will Munson and the big-company goons who try to siphon off his water. Even the tiniest roles are played by gifted actors with classically Western faces – James Handy, Lennie Loftin – and there's a sort of sepia tone to John Mathieson's cinematography, giving the whole a sense of breathed-in reality and old-fashioned heft. There is CG here, of course, but it's sparse and largely invisible. As the opening pages of Mangold, Scott Frank and Michael Green's script says, this will not be a "hyper-choreographed, gravity-defying, city-block destroying CG f***fest"; the biggest action set-piece takes place in a forest, far from civilization, and features just a few vehicles and perhaps a score of unfortunate goons. And the most dazzling effect is the appearance of Logan clone X-24, the animalistic, ruthless alter-ego that is everything Logan fears about himself.

The high stakes are emotional then, rather than built on extinction-level events. Across a thousand miles of desert and farmland, Logan continues to deny the obvious fact that he cares for Charles and Laura; all too conscious of the truth he keeps repeating, "Bad shit happens to people I care about." Even people he only meets briefly, like the Munsons. But when Laura shoots back at him, "Then I'll be fine," there's a sense that he's shaken out of his pose. And of course, he does care; of course, there's still a shred of goodness underneath that can power one last burst of heroics.

In the end, Logan dies defending not just a bunch of innocent kids but the hope for a mutant future, and that feels right. "So this is what it feels like," says Logan as he goes, referring not just to death itself but also, says Mangold, to holding the hand of someone he loves as Laura weeps at his side. There's a sense of redemption for him in the end, in the man who always feared his own capacity for violence but who gives up his life for a noble cause. He's buried under a cairn high in the mountains, with an X to mark his grave. No gunslinger ever had a better send-off.

X-MEN: ORIGINS WOLVERINE AND THE WOLVERINE

The first Wolverine film was – pretty much everyone agrees – a mess. Jackman's never bad, but there were dozens of extraneous mutants in what was supposed to be a leaner, meaner X-spin-off from promising director Gavin Hood. And never forget what they did to Wade Wilson, sewing up his mouth and delaying a Deadpool movie by a full decade. Mangold's *The Wolverine* was considerably better, putting the focus on Logan and taking the action to Japan to follow Frank Miller and Chris Claremont's classic arc. But a too-big, too-CG ending once again left the fans feeling unsatisfied. Happily, director James Mangold clearly agreed with them.

SPIDER-MAN: HOMECOMING

WE DEFINITELY DIDN'T NEED ANOTHER SPIDER-MAN REBOOT IN 2017. IT WAS JUST

FIVE YEARS SINCE THE DO-OVER, WHICH CAME ONLY FIVE YEARS AFTER THE FIRST

TRILOGY CLOSED.

But after painting the *Amazing* films into a corner by killing Gwen Stacey, Sony teamed up with the MCU to work together on a new and better Webslinger. And as soon as we saw Tom Holland's Peter Parker in *Captain America: Civil War*, audiences realized that we definitely did need another Spider-Man after all. So what went right?

The killer is that Holland has all the wide-eyed optimism of the comics' Peter Parker but a new, millennial edge of competence and unashamed geekery that make him instantly endearing. The other two Peter Parkers were fine actors, but this time, something just clicked. Holland's version is desperate to keep everyone

happy, from his aunt to Tony Stark, but also to do the right thing, even against petty street crime; he really puts the "friendly" and "neighbourhood" into "friendly neighbourhood Spider-Man".

For the supporting cast, director Jon Watts took inspiration from the 1980s teen movies of John Hughes and pulled together a gaggle of eccentric, fascinating teen characters. Peter's best friend, Ned

Opposite Our friendly neighbourhood Spider-Man takes in the sights.

Below Peter Parker (Tom Holland) works to save the world with best mate Ned (Jacob Batalon) in shop class.

(Jacob Batalon), swiftly discovers his superhero identity and dives into the fun aspects of his friend's double life. Peter's crush, Liz (Laura Harrier), is also an academic decathlete and not just a knockout; his sort-of friend Michelle (Zendaya) is so cool that you can't ever predict what she's going to say and wouldn't dare guess. And the bully, Flash Thompson (Tony Revoloni), is now a snarky rich kid who makes up names, rather than a hulking bruiser. It all feels more natural than the tired high-school clichés we've seen before. It also feels modern: even when Marisa Tomei's very cool Aunt May finds Peter half-naked with Ned, there's no gay panic or crass jokes.

The bad guy, Michael Keaton's Vulture, is also different. Sam Raimi had tried to include Vulture but he wasn't popular with the studio at that time; luckily for us, times changed. A hard-working guy who just wants to provide for his family seems to fit a post-financial crash era, and the original Batman offered the right blend of charm and menace to keep things interesting. That's aside from the reveal of his *other* identity: one of the best twists in any superhero movie and an eloquent argument for colour-blind casting, even aside from its obvious moral advantages.

Frankly, you'd be happy watching this mix of characters just going about their day without any superheroics. The reason that Watts had the luxury of spending time with them and injecting humour and heart into the story was that Marvel and Sony gave themselves a box-office head start by including Robert Downey Jr's Tony Stark. Their quasi-father-and-son relationship neatly replaces the oft-told Uncle Ben dynamic, but this way we don't have to see his origin *again* or kill any likeable older men. It gives Peter a limit to butt up against, making him seem more puppyish and less powerful than he otherwise might, and softens Tony's considerable edges.

And it's funny. Really funny – in Michelle's asides, Captain America's cringe-worthy educational videos and Peter's desperate attempts to cover his secret life. You buy this character as both a hero and a kid; you believe that he could either spend his evening on a Lego Death Star *or* stopping super-criminals, and it doesn't even feel like a contradiction. Thanks only in part to Holland's age and more to his talent, this incarnation feels fresh and bounces with unrestrained energy. Skipping over the origin story we already know also helps.

Finally, the film has smart things to say about what it

Above Spidey with mentor Tony Stark (Robert Downey Jr) and handler Happy (Jon Favreau).

Right *Homecoming*'s MJ, played by Zendaya, offered a new twist on the character.

Opposite Michael Keaton plays the Vulture, the illegal weapons dealer who Spider-Man must take down.

means to be a hero. It's genuinely important and mildly revolutionary that Peter's decathlon team wins without his help: not everyone is waiting around for Peter to save them, particularly not Michelle or Liz. Too many films try to make their heroes indispensable in every way instead of only the necessary ones. The later moment (ripped from the comics) where Peter is buried under a huge weight of concrete and gives in to justifiable panic and pain for an instant is deeply upsetting: for all his great powers, this is still just a young person in distress.

As it turns out, Peter's path to heroism is littered with failures, and his final victory comes at a steep cost to himself and a friend. Great responsibility sometimes bites. When Peter turns down the chance to join the Avengers at the end, it's a surer sign that he's ready than Tony's invitation. He would soon step up to the big league, to a place that he earned.

BLACK PANTHER

THE SAD FACT ABOUT COMIC-BOOK MOVIES IS THAT THERE ARE MORE MAJOR
SUPERHEROES PLAYED BY SANDY-HAIRED WHITE ACTORS CALLED CHRIS THAN
THERE ARE BY BLACK OR FEMALE STARS.

But representation matters: every child deserves the chance to grow up and feel that they could fight, or fly, or save the world. So when you see little kids in London throwing snowballs and shouting, "Wakanda forever!" after seeing *Black Panther*, it's clear that it has achieved something important; that they have a role model unlike any they have seen before. If that were all *Black Panther* offered, it would be enough. But it does so much more. This film takes extraordinary risks with the superhero genre, making its villain profoundly sympathetic in his aims and its hero complicit in a wrong that goes back centuries.

Black Panther – that name pre-dated the African-American community movement of the 1960s and 1970s – was created in early 1966, and despite previous efforts in the 1990s, a film never quite came to pass. Superheroes had always belonged in America. They projected their power into other countries, sometimes, but place their origin anywhere else and you seemed to get mystics and magicians, rather

Opposite The Black Panther prepares to strike.

Below T'Challa (Chadwick Boseman) fights for the kingship of Wakanda against Erik 'Killmonger' Stevens (Michael B. Jordan).

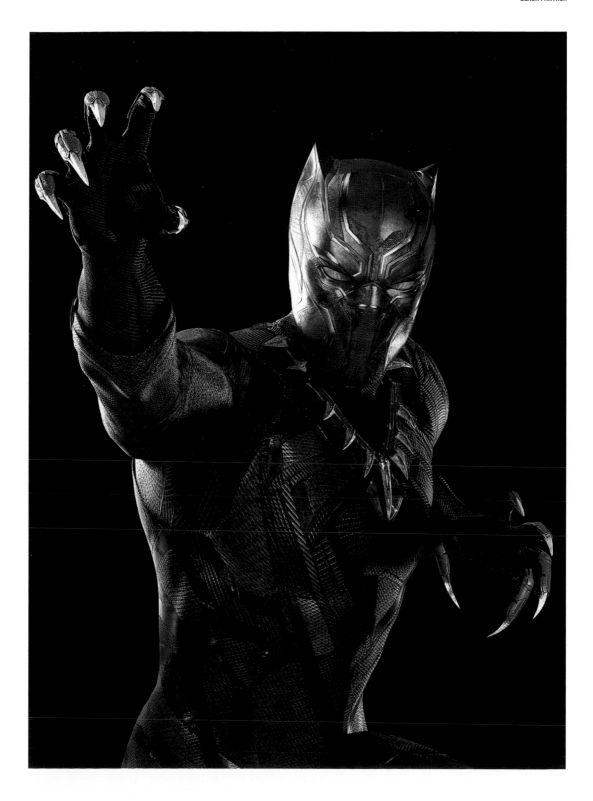

than muscle-bound Adonii. Hollywood couldn't get its head around the idea of an African hero, and even the scripts developed during that time took a sort of *Coming To America* approach to the African prince brought to the United States.

What Marvel and director Ryan Coogler realized is that it's possible to build another world – to create a vision of an Africa that never fell under colonialist rule and imagine the wonders it might achieve. So we get this Afro-futurist Wakanda. It apes the traditional dress, weaponry and architecture of peoples all over the African continent (accents too; they wander a *lot*) but possesses technology far beyond the self-satisfied global north. They distil the best aspects of hundreds of cultures, but this idealism is no more dreamlike than *Superman* or *Captain America*. Wakanda exposes the lie that Africa is inevitably impoverished – and the joy on Okoye's (Danai Gurira) face as she announces "We're home" is the expression of a vast diaspora finding a haven where their civilization was never attacked. This film offers a profound homecoming.

Above Laetitia Wright as tech genius (and T'Challa's sister) Shuri.

Opposite Winston Duke had a breakout performance as M'Baku, the warlike head of Wakanda's Mountain tribe.

Chadwick Boseman's T'Challa/Black Panther, at the head of this kingdom, is a nuanced hero. "You're a good man, with a good heart, and it's hard for a good man to be king," says his father, T'Chaka (John Kani), when T'Challa visits the ancestral plane to see his ancestors. There's a touch of *Hamlet* as T'Challa grapples with his father's imperfect legacy and his own responsibilities. Should he project Wakandan power outward to protect the descendants of slaves still suffering the toxic, racist effects of that legacy? Or should he maintain his country's tradition of non-intervention and keep his people safe in their isolation? He is torn; his would-be girlfriend, Nakia (Lupita Nyong'o), and closest male friend, W'Kabi (Daniel Kaluuya), favour reaching out, while his closest advisor, Okoye, is more cautious.

Into this uncertain time come agents provocateurs in Andy Serkis's Ulysses Klaue (glimpsed in *Age of Ultron*) and, most devastatingly, Michael B. Jordan's Erik Killmonger/N'Jadaka. Killmonger seeks to avenge his father's death at T'Chaka's hands, but also the throne, so he can redress the global balance of racial power. "The sun will never set on the Wakandan Empire," he proclaims, echoing the boast made of Queen Victoria's British domains. Coogler's spinning camera shot as Killmonger takes the throne reflects the disorientation he brings; he turns Wakanda upside down and brings all its dirty secrets to light.

Killmonger's argument is not unsympathetic, and he ultimately succeeds in opening the country up (though not as radically as he had hoped). In fact, in plot terms, you'd need few changes to make Killmonger a hero; he'd need to kill fewer people and wouldn't shoot his girlfriend (Nabiyah Be's Linda). In personality, however, he has serious issues. He has become infected with a very hawkish and, ironically, imperialist sense that he has the right to meddle in the affairs of other countries.

The film climaxes in a minor Wakandan civil war for the future of the country's soul, turning female royal guards the Dora Milaje against the Border Tribe and dividing a happy couple when Okoye and W'Kabi find themselves on opposite sides. But no one truly wins. T'Challa offers to save Killmonger; the latter chooses death instead. "Just bury me in the ocean with my ancestors who jumped from the ships because they knew death was better than bondage," he says – an astonishingly powerful kiss-off line for a star of a Hollywood movie.

Even aside from its powerful message, there are delightful moments in this film. Okoye steals every scene in which she appears, and the near identical side-eye that she and T'Challa give Martin Freeman's Everett Ross when he blithely tries to take control of the situation is masterful. The "Tolkien white guys", as the internet dubbed them, are the butt of many jokes: Shuri calls Ross "colonizer" as a throwaway diss, and M'Baku (Winston Duke) merely huffs at him like a gorilla. Klaue is a little more clued up, but still not enough to know what he's dealing with in Killmonger. The joke's on him.

After winning Marvel its first three Oscars (for Best Costume, Production Design and Score) and taking $700 million in the US alone and almost as much again worldwide, *Black Panther* proved itself beyond any reasonable expectation. The question will be whether Hollywood takes this as a sign that they should take more risks and be just as daring in the future, rooting their heroes in closely observed cultures from around the world; challenging the cinematic assumption that the US is the centre of the world and making such explicitly political statements. *Black Panther* may feature a man wearing cat ears, but it is a superhero film that could, in small ways, change the world.

TEEN TITANS GO!
TO THE MOVIES

NO DISRESPECT TO *DEADPOOL 2*, BUT THE BEST SUPERHERO SATIRE OF 2018 WAS
THIS MANIC ANIMATED EFFORT. *TEEN TITANS GO! TO THE MOVIES* THUMBS ITS NOSE AT
DC, MARVEL AND THE VERY IDEA OF THE HOLLYWOOD SUPERHERO MOVIE.

It even has one of the best Stan Lee cameos ever recorded, despite the fact that he works for the other guys, and it saw Nicolas Cage finally play Superman 20 years after the idea was first mooted. So how did it all go right?

The Teen Titans started off as a sidekick supergroup: a line-up of largely second-string DC characters led by Batman's young counterpart, Robin. The comic has come and gone over the years with various line-ups, but its modern popularity dates back to the early noughties cartoon action series. That was revived in 2013 as *Teen Titans Go!*, a silly comedy with the same characters: Robin, Raven (the daughter of a demon), Cyborg (part-machine), Beast Boy (can turn into animals) and Starfire (super-powered alien who likes hugs). This is the kind of gang that has a theme tune

Below The Titans in typically serious and heroic form.

Opposite Robin (Scott Menville) accosts Batman (Jimmy Kimmel – seriously) on the red carpet of his latest film.

celebrating their own powers, but who accidentally allow the bad guys to escape while they're singing it.

For the first 15 minutes or so, you might wonder what on earth is going on and why you're watching this inane Saturday-morning kid's show. There's simplistic animation and fart gags as the Titans battle a giant pink monster ("The inflated destroyer, Balloon Man") and squabble among themselves. But then the plot kicks in: Robin, frustrated by the premiere of yet another Batman film, decides that the one thing he wants in life is his own movie, and the Titans set out to secure one. By any means necessary.

The genius stroke of this story is that it looks fun and peppy but is also deeply twisted. The Titans attempt to ensure their place in cinema history by removing every other superhero from existence, which is... extreme. They time-travel to save Krypton (via the power of electronic dance music) so that Superman will never leave; direct the Wayne parents away from their appointment with destiny; and guide four small turtles away from a puddle of ooze. Their solution to the existence of Aquaman is too delightfully awful to spoil in print. But when they return to the present and find it a wasteland, they just as quickly doom Superman's homeworld once more and push Batman's parents down Crime Alley to their deaths, giving young Bruce a thumbs-up as

they go. "Well, altering the space-time continuum didn't work. Who saw that coming?" marvels Cyborg. It would be monstrous if it weren't so hilarious – and it's hard to condemn anyone whose time machine is a tricycle "powered by radness".

What makes this work is the mix of extremely childish comedy with wide-ranging cleverness. There's deep comic-book knowledge (an appearance from the deeply obscure *Challengers of the Unknown*), inspired film gags (a *Lion King* dream sequence; the *Back to the Future* theme accompanying time-travel) and cheeky digs (a Shia LaBeouf gag, the line "I think his dad's a cop!"). We've had enough superhero movies to enjoy these riffs on the excesses of the genre, with Batman growling, "What's your mother's name?" at Superman as the fake studio rain pours down, or the Titans throwing Superman a "Kryptonite party". And the idea that Warner Bros might make an Alfred

Top the Justice League line up: Green Lantern (Lil Yachty), Wonder Woman (Halsey), Superman (Nicolas Cage), Batman and Flash (Wil Wheaton).

Opposite The Titans: Starfire (Hynden Walch), Robin, Beast Boy (Greg Cipes), Cyborg (Khary Payton) and Raven (Tara Strong).

movie before they make a Robin one is not so far-fetched, given that prequel TV show *Pennyworth* premiered in 2019. Admittedly, the Batmobile and Utility Belt movies remain a tiny bit more far-fetched. At the time of writing, at least.

There's a nut of genuine concern here that superhero films are deforming comic-books; that the only heroes who matter now are those who make it to the big screen. But effectively, you have to really *want* to see a deeper meaning amid all this joyful anarchy. Everything else is secondary to the gags, the bright colours and the insanely catchy songs. With the best last line of the year and that music, this'll leave you feeling upbeat.

THE LEGO BATMAN MOVIE

These two films are not strictly related, aside from the fact that they're both animated, both feature voice work by Will Arnett and are made by Warner Bros. But they share a commitment to the absurd, a deep love of the comic-book characters they lampoon and a message about learning to work with others instead of shooting for individual glory. Arnett's preening, self-important and blithely clueless Batman is a comic creation for the ages, and yet he's really not that far off his more serious brethren. Perhaps you don't need to try too hard to turn a man in a bat suit into a joke.

THE ROUND-UP

GIVEN THE AMOUNT OF MONEY AND CARE LAVISHED ON THEM, MOST SUPERHERO FILMS TURN OUT TO BE AT LEAST OK. BUT ALL THAT MONEY OFTEN COMES WITH STUDIO INTERFERENCE AND RIGID EXPECTATIONS OF THE FILM THAT SHOULD RESULT, AND THAT CAN MAKE FILMS THAT FEEL A LITTLE COOKIE-CUTTER. THEN THERE ARE THE EFFORTS THAT STICK TO THEIR WEIRD AND WONDERFUL GUNS BUT NEVER GET AS BIG AN AUDIENCE AS THEY DESERVE. HERE'S A ROUND-UP OF THAT SELECTION.

FANTASTIC FOUR AND
RISE OF THE SILVER SURFER

Tim Story's take on "Marvel's first family" has a breezy, family-friendly tone. Michael Chiklis's The Thing is the standout: a tragically rock-formed bruiser, but Chris Evans' Human Torch makes a likeable dude-bro (hey, this guy makes a good superhero!); Jessica Alba is the quiet but determined Invisible Woman, and Ioan Gruffudd the stalwart(ish) leader. The problem is their collective chemistry is off. The cosmically tinged sequel, with Laurence Fishburne voicing the titular herald of Galactus, is bigger but not significantly better.

DAREDEVIL

Ben Affleck's first stab at superheroics is better than it is often credited: the cast is great (particularly Colin Farrell) and the effects of Daredevil's radar-like "vision" are beautifully conceived in the rain scenes. But director Mark Steven Johnson never quite settled on the film's tone, pinballing between grim solemnity and a lighter, jokier touch that belongs to something much lighter and younger-skewing. In the light of the much better Netflix show, it now looks seriously dated.

BATMAN: THE MOVIE

Adam West's Batman must save world leaders from the combined attentions of all his biggest villains in this big-screen version of the classic TV show. As you'd expect, it's a gloriously camp affair, with its Bat-shark repellent and heroic dolphins (really). Having Robin fall in love with a disguised Catwoman (Lee Meriweather) is inspired, and the bizarre plot that sees world leaders "dehydrated" into small piles of dust is a giggle. Plus it makes a fascinating double-bill with *The Dark Knight* – *these two* are the same character...?!

CAPTAIN UNDERPANTS: THE FIRST EPIC MOVIE

Sure, this is not your typical superhero film, but it is a strangely delightful little animation about two schoolboys who hypnotize their mean school principal, Mr Krupp, into becoming the superhero star of their comic-strip, *Captain Underpants*. When supervillain Professor Poopypants comes to town, only the Captain can save the day. Voiced by Kevin Hart, Thomas Middleditch, Nick Kroll and Ed Helms, this is not a mature movie, sure, but its meta-humour and invention make it a far better watch than you would expect.

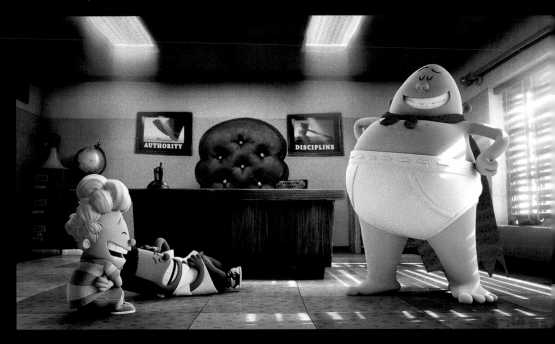

TEENAGE MUTANT NINJA TURTLES
AND SEQUELS

The cartoon show was a massive hit in the 1980s, so a live-action film was the obvious next step, particularly at a time when *Batman* had just broken cinema records. Jim Henson oversaw the creation of the Turtles' suits, which were impressive pieces of work, and the first movie, at least, had real heart and humour as well as pizza gags, ninja fights and sewers. But the dark, grungy cinematography did the film's look no favours, and there's ultimately only so much expression you can get from foam rubber. The first film was a huge hit despite its handicaps, but two sequels – 1991's *The Secret of the Ooze* and 1993's *Teenage Mutant Ninja Turtles III* – saw steadily diminishing returns.

TMNT

It's not clear who, precisely, asked for a darker, CG-assisted take on the Turtles, but we got one anyway from director Jonathan Liebesman – previously a horror guy – and producer Michael Bay. Somehow, the CG characters were further from the cartoons than their men-in-suits predecessors, but at least it made for slightly faster and more fluid action. This was another box-office hit and also spawned a (less successful) sequel, *Out of the Shadows*.

THE AMAZING SPIDER-MAN AND AMAZING SPIDER-MAN 2

A mere five years after the last one, Spider-Man was rebooted and sent back to high school to face, as it turned out, the Lizard (Rhys Ifans). Andrew Garfield and Emma Stone, as Peter Parker and Gwen Stacey, are well cast and as adorable as a basket full of baby unicorn kittens, but there's little else here that stands out. And when they killed Gwen Stacey in the sequel (why didn't they just call her MJ?), there was nowhere left to go.

SUPERMAN RETURNS

A sequel, technically, to *Superman II* that simply ignores the two films in between. Brandon Routh makes an excellent Christopher Reeve substitute and there's real reverence for those early films, but the plot is just a frame for Superman to lift an increasingly heavy series of things. The idea that Superman has a son, thanks to that whole "being human" interlude in the earlier film, is interesting but underdeveloped. Still, it's visually beautiful and hearing the John Williams theme again would melt the hardest of hearts.

GHOST RIDER AND
GHOST RIDER: SPIRIT OF VENGEANCE

A stunt rider makes a deal with the devil to save his father's life, only for his dad to die in a tragic accident anyway. And so young Johnny Blaze (Nicolas Cage) becomes a demon with a fiery head, which is nominative determinism at its finest. There's a lot of cool effects here – as in the second film where the Ghost Rider uses his hell-powers on a massive strip-mining vehicle, or when Sam Elliott turns up as another Ghost Rider – but neither film has a great villain and they're both a little too self-serious. The *Agents of S.H.I.E.L.D.* version, made when the rights reverted to Marvel, is more fun.

VENOM

Tom Hardy leaves Bane behind for another large and misshapen creature, as his hothead photographer Eddie Brock becomes infected with the symbiotic alien, Venom. An odd mix of gore, fish-out-of-water comedy and traditional superheroics ensued – something different enough to prove a huge hit at the box-office (although not with critics). Hardy is likeable and immensely game, which helps, and if it has the feel of an early noughties throwback, perhaps there's joy in that nostalgia.

AQUAMAN

THERE'S A LOT TO LOVE IN JAMES WAN'S *AQUAMAN*, BUT THERE'S ALSO JUST A LOT. THIS IS A FILM THAT FLINGS EVERYTHING AT THE SCREEN TO SEE WHAT STICKS, WITH LITTLE THOUGHT FOR COHERENCE OR NARRATIVE FORM IN THE END RESULT. IT'S JACKSON POLLOCK STORYTELLING: PERHAPS SPLASHING AND DRIPPING SEEMED APPROPRIATE, GIVEN THE FILM'S MILIEU. THE END RESULT LOOKS GREAT ON YOUR WALL BUT IS IT, Y'KNOW, ART?

The decision to cast Jason Momoa as Arthur Curry / Aquaman was made way back in *Batman V Superman*, and by 2018 when this came out everyone recognized the hulking Hawaiian as a great fit for the half-human Prince of Atlantis. Amber Heard had already been saddled with a Little Mermaid wig and catsuit as water-witch Mera in her brief *Justice League* appearance, though her look gets a rejig here. But Wan cast Temuera Morrison and Nicole Kidman as Arthur's parents; Yahya Abdul-Mateen II as his aggrieved enemy Manta; Willem Dafoe as his mentor Vulko and Patrick Wilson as King Orm, holder of the throne of Atlantis. They're solid choices, but the problem is that all these characters require loads of plot when we could just be watching Momoa punch, flirt with or shout at things. That would be much more fun than watching Wilson struggle to make an impact past his own CG suit and Dafoe wonder why he's there.

So there's a revenge plot for Manta, a power-consolidation quest for Orm and a riddle for Aquaman and Mera to solve in order to save the world – plus layered flashbacks and frequent lectures on the rules of Atlantean society from Vulka and Mera (whose name is apparently short for "Princess Merely-Around For Exposition"). The themes hidden amid all this noise concern legacy, and family ties, and breaking with toxic traditions. Arthur scorns Atlantis' sexist and cruel laws, knowing the hardship they caused in his own life, but there's a sense that he really wants everyone to just get along so he can return to a life of hard work and hard drinking rather than governance. Even by the end of the film there's little sense that he's going to spend time in committee sorting things out. Orm wants to assert Atlantis' superior tech and, essentially, take over the world to stop humanity's polluting instincts – though that's barely discussed after a few throwaway remarks early on.

That's not out of character: the film barely pauses to consider any ideas or even explain what's happening. A global tidal wave, unleashed by Atlantis, causes devastation in the opening scenes and is never mentioned again. The bad guy engineers a false-flag attack by humanity, but that falls by the wayside too. Wan is too busy dazzling us with the vast potential of the world beneath the waves. At one point we travel through a *Pitch Black* tribute into a Lost World straight out of Jules Verne, before detouring to chat

Above A fully shredded Jason Momoa decked out in complete Aquaman gear.

with a monstrous leviathan voiced by Julie Andrews and fight a battle alongside the crab people. And at no point during this journey does anyone express much astonishment or even pause to say, "This is a bit odd, isn't it?". Octopuses drum and sharks roar (sharks *roar*??) and little of it rewards concentration, but it's a lot of fun to watch. Wan – not only a horror veteran but director of one of the best *Fast & Furious* movies, the seventh – is rightly confident in his action directing and he finds endless variety and shade in the fight scenes. But it verges on too much even before everything culminates in a gigantic, *Lord of the Rings*-esque fantasy battle on the seabed.

Still, you can't accuse them of failing to entertain us with something we've never seen before. Really, the only shortcoming that matters is the failure to capitalize on its own hero. Momoa's a roguish delight, yet he spends much of the film trailing behind Mera, having stuff explained to him, rather than showing why his name is the title. We have to hope that the planned sequel will give him considerably more room to work with, and give us an Aquaman who fully meets his potential.

Above Not many films can say they feature Willem Dafoe riding an armoured shark. *Aquaman* can.

Opposite Amber Heard's look as Mera received an overhaul following her *Justice League* appearance.

Below Nicole Kidman looks the part as an ocean queen. If only she'd had more to do.

THE BEST SUPER-CASTING

AS MANY DIRECTORS HAVE FOUND, THESE FILMS LIVE OR DIE ON THEIR CASTING. FIND THE RIGHT SUPREMELY FIT AND GORGEOUS STAR AND YOU CAN MAKE A BILLION; GET IT WRONG AND YOU CAN GO DOWN IN HISTORY AS CATWOMAN. WHAT YOU NEED IS A STRANGE ALCHEMY, SOMEONE WHO IS EITHER CLOSE TO THE CHARACTER'S ESSENCE (CHRIS EVANS' CAPTAIN AMERICA, FOR INSTANCE) OR WHO LOOKS SO GOOD THAT NO ONE QUESTIONS IT (GAL GADOT, WHO SURELY IS WONDER WOMAN MASQUERADING AS ONE OF US). WE'VE ALREADY LOOKED AT THE BAD GUYS, BUT HERE WE LOOK AT THE SUPERHEROES SO PERFECTLY SUITED THAT THEY BECAME SUPERSTARS.

HUGH JACKMAN, WOLVERINE/LOGAN
JAMES HOWLETT
X-MEN SERIES, *WOLVERINE* SERIES

He's a foot too tall and several miles too genial, yet Hugh Jackman is, by near universal acclaim, the perfect Wolverine. This from a guy who spends most of his off-time on Broadway singing, or reviving the movie musical as *The Greatest Showman*. Perhaps it's a Jekyll-and-Hyde scenario, in which he pours all the aggression he fails to use in his daily life into the role; perhaps it's a case of opposites attracting. But even when his films have underperformed, Jackman has managed to convince us that he's a short, amnesiac berserker with claws in his hands.

RYAN REYNOLDS, DEADPOOL
DEADPOOL SERIES

It took several tries to get it right for Ryan Reynolds. He was too handsome, too charming and too athletic *not* to play a superhero, yet nothing seemed to stick. Hannibal King was OK, but the film sucked. Wade Wilson should have worked, but his arc was horribly fumbled. And *Green Lantern*, well, it left him isolated in a sea of CG madness.

But *Deadpool*, at last, proved an uncannily good fit, allowing the quippy Canadian to cut loose and make the Merc with the Mouth his own. Reynolds' role in everything from script to marketing helped to make Deadpool the sensation that he is, and upped the filth levels in superhero films by 17 per cent, singlehandedly.

HAYLEY ATWELL, AGENT PEGGY CARTER

CAPTAIN AMERICA SERIES, *AGENT CARTER*, *AVENGERS: AGE OF ULTRON*

There are far too few great roles for women in comic-book films, but Hayley Atwell took the little she was given and ran with it. Her Agent Carter is a lone woman in a sea of testosterone, and one sufficiently formidable to more than hold her own. Through the films and the TV show, she is constantly stymied and blocked by men who underestimate her, but when she's given room to act, this woman gets results – like spotting Steve Rogers' potential early (they bond over their shared underdog status), or founding S.H.I.E.L.D. Impressive composure and undeniable pluck can take you a long way in life, but it's her brain that's the key to Carter's success.

CHRISTOPHER REEVE, SUPERMAN/CLARK KENT
SUPERMAN SERIES

The longest and most comprehensive casting search in superhero history – even the producer's wife's dentist did a screentest – led, inevitably, to one man. He wasn't a star, not then; it was only his second film. But Christopher Reeve never wavered for a moment in his commitment to *Superman*, and even when conflicted or confused, somehow seemed steady and trustworthy. It's also an impressive display of acting craft when he switches his body language from god to geek, transforming from Big Blue Boy Scout to fumbling Clark Kent. Neither Routh nor Cavill, who followed him, have been poor, but Reeve remains the gold-standard by whom other Supermen are judged.

WESLEY SNIPES, BLADE
BLADE TRILOGY

OK, so he went off the boil by the third film, but Wesley Snipes's Blade is a superb match of star and character. He gave the Daywalker focus, intensity and the ability to stalk around in an ankle-length leather trench coat without looking ridiculous. He made superheroes cool again. And he showed a martial-arts prowess that few of those who followed him have been able to match. Snipes's casting as Blade, and the responsibility he took to make the character great, kick-started the modern superhero era, and he deserves more credit for that than he gets.

SCARLETT JOHANSSON, NATASHA ROMANOV
IRON MAN 2, CAPTAIN AMERICA SERIES, AVENGERS SERIES

This is a less universally acclaimed piece of casting, but Scarlett Johansson has done a lot with very little as the Russian assassin turned S.H.I.E.L.D. operative and Avenger. She created, from almost nothing, a sense of long trust and friendship with colleagues such as Captain America and Hawkeye. She has an air of reserve and wariness in her friendships, and she holds back a lot, but she also shows real loyalty and a knack for getting through to difficult people (*see Civil War*, for example). At long last, she'll have her own film, we're told, in Marvel's *Phase Four*. It's long overdue.

MICHELLE PFEIFFER, CATWOMAN
BATMAN RETURNS

No one, ever, has been as simultaneously hot and cool as this Catwoman. The moment when Michelle Pfeiffer cartwheels out of a department store and stops in front of Batman and the Penguin to drawl a casual "Miaow" as the building explodes behind her is a display of god-level attitude. Her louche, slouching elegance and utter disregard for anyone else is perfectly feline and brilliantly effective, as is her transformation from the mousey, stuttering Selina Kyle into the Latex-clad anti-heroine. Anne Hathaway managed a worthy follow-up, but there is only one true Catwoman.

ROBERT DOWNEY JR, TONY STARK/IRON MAN

IRON MAN AND *AVENGERS* SERIES,
SPIDER-MAN: HOMECOMING

It's a sad cliché to note that Downey Jr is well cast as Tony Stark, and yet there is no getting around it. The formerly wastrel son of a successful father, the huge talent who didn't always appreciate what he had, the good-for-nothing who turned it all around yet who remains eccentric and unpredictable... it's hard to see how it could have been anyone else. But the first of the Avengers to be cast also set the tone for his entire cinematic universe. These guys would laugh in the face of danger even as they sweated to avert it, and would labour tirelessly to correct their own mistakes and become better people. It's inspiring to watch.

SPIDER-MAN:
INTO THE SPIDER-VERSE

IT'S NO MEAN FEAT THAT, IN THE YEAR OF *BLACK PANTHER* AND *INFINITY WAR*, THE

MOST GARLANDED AND HIGHLY- ACCLAIMED SUPERHERO FILM CAME FROM

SONY ANIMATION.

The Oscar, BAFTA, Golden Globe and Annie-winning *Spider-Man: Into The Spider-Verse* has a strong claim to be not only the best *Spider-Man* film yet (in a crowded field) but one of the most innovative animations ever. It mixes CG animation and hand-drawn touches; uncanny realism and glorious cartooniness; emotional realism and broad, blockbuster entertainment. It's practically perfect.

Our arachnid hero this time is *not* Peter Parker but the Ultimate Comics universe's Spider-Man, Afro-Latino teenager Miles Morales (voiced flawlessly by Shameik Moore). He's a gifted kid struggling to fit into the science academy where he has won a

place, often sneaking away to spend time with his cool, undemanding uncle Aaron (Mahershala Ali). But after he's bitten by a strange looking spider and grows several inches overnight, Morales develops uncanny powers and... well, you can guess. He meets his universe's Peter Parker (Chris Pine) and they immediately sense their connection, delighting in one another's existence.

Opposite Miles' initial forays into superheroism aren't quite the accomplished feats we've come to expect.

Below The film is never afraid to burst out into a radical colour palette at a moment's notice..

Above Peter B. Parker, Spider-Gwen and Miles all experience a familiar tingling.

Opposite Every frame of *Into the Spider-Verse* is imbued with breathtaking style and detail.

But they meet during a knock-down, drag-out fight with a significant portion of Parker's rogues gallery, and even as Spidey tries to protect and advise his young counterpart he is pulled away. "I always get up," Parker tells Morales, after he's knocked to the floor. Alas, this time the Kingpin (Liev Schreiber) puts him down permanently. Morales is left grieving, alone and understandably terrified. Unlike Peter, he never had time to revel in his powers before this horror, and he is adrift – at least until he learns that the same danger that killed his predecessor created a dimensional portal and drew in other Spider-persons who could offer guidance. Unfortunately for Morales, the first one he meets is the schlubby, washed-up Peter B. Parker (Jake Johnston), who is not immediately reassuring. "Everyone knows that the best way to learn is under intense, life-threatening pressure," is about typical of his mentoring style.

It's worth noting that Miles, unlike so many other superheroes and most of these Spider-peers, is not an orphan. He has a supportive and loving family, but in a mixed-up world and amid the turmoil of adolescence, that is not always enough. Even with that secure home and his many gifts, it requires time, mentoring and huge personal courage for Miles to become Spider-Man in his own right. It will take a leap of faith, in the end, and the resilience to stand up again no matter how many times he gets hit – as both Peters tell him. So the challenge for Morales is learning to overcome his natural diffidence and self-doubt and stand up for what he believes. His family ties into that question, because that's a message very deliberately in keeping with themes of African-American civil rights and empowerment as well as superheroism. "Our family doesn't run from things, Miles," says his mother Rio

(Luna Lauren Velez), while his father emphasizes responsibility and self-respect. Even with that help, risking your life to do the right thing is a challenge for any kid, particularly one smart enough to have a sense of self-preservation.

These are huge themes, yet this is not a heavy, dour film: the Spider-people see to that. Hailee Steinfeld's wary Spider-Gwen is hesitant to make new friends after losing her in-universe bestie Peter Parker, but she and Morales bond all the same. Johnston's Parker is hilariously hang-dog ("Never invest in a spider-themed restaurant") and likeably under-achieving, at least by the standards of this company. And the three more exotic Spideys are endless fun. There's the futuristic, manga-esque Peni Parker and her robot-suited pet spider; John Mulaney's delightfully *Looney Tunes* Peter Porker / Spider-Ham, a cartoon spider bitten by a radioactive pig; and Nicolas Cage's Spider-Man Noir, trench coat permanently billowing around him ("Wherever I go, the wind follows, and the wind... smells like rain").

There's so much glory in the details. If you didn't know that Kathryn Hahn's gleefully malevolent Livia Octavius was a bad guy, you might guess from her horrifically cluttered computer desktop – and you might wonder why Lily Tomlin's Aunt May calls her "Liv", a moniker Octavius says is reserved for friends. There are meta touches (when Spider-Hamm bids farewell, sadly, with, "That's all folks", Peter B. Parker wonders, "Is he allowed to say that? Legally?"). But this never becomes just an empty, self-referential yuk fest.

The traditional Stan Lee cameo is a moving one, and the soundtrack is packed with bangers.

Miles Morales' journey to superhero status looks and sounds like nothing you have ever seen, remixing our comic-book expectations in every way. Daniel Pemberton's hyper-flexible score punctuates the action and shifts endlessly from flashes of hip-hop cool to unexpected, metallic horror (listen for the Prowler's theme, the best bad-guy riff since *The Winter Soldier*) to orchestral lushness. The animation is equally fluid. Instead of the usual red / cyan / yellow colour scheme this plays with magenta / neon blue / orange, sometimes enlivened with fuschia and a kind of Kryptonite green. Comic-book captions and thought-bubbles pop up; there are black outlines where normal animation would have none, or red-and-green 3D outlines where you'd expect black – not for a stereoscopic effect but just because it looks unsettling and also beautiful. The bad guys are animated in different ways too, sometimes offering a match-up to their Spider-foes. It all suggests that reality itself is malleable, changing with our hero's moods, reflecting his actions and adding infinite depth to the picture.

In other words, *Into The Spider-Verse* uses the full power of animation and a huge breadth of superhero lore to bring its characters to life. Then it tells a powerful story about becoming a fully realized person in the world, someone who will fight for a better future no matter how scared they feel. It's not enough to have powers, this film tells us. It's how you use them that matters.

CAPTAIN MARVEL

IT TOOK THE MCU (SEE PAGE 66) A NEARLY UNFORGIVEABLE 21 FILMS TO MAKE ONE WITH A SOLO FEMALE LEAD. AT LEAST WHEN THEY BELATEDLY GOT AROUND TO IT, THEY DID NOT THROW AWAY THEIR SHOT. BRIE LARSON'S CAROL DANVERS IS AN EXPLICITLY FEMINIST HERO, WHO ADDRESSES SPECIFIC FEMALE EXPERIENCES, IN A WAY THAT SHOWS IMMEDIATELY WHAT SHE HAS TO OFFER THE CROWDED MARVEL UNIVERSE.

This woman is not a cheap male fantasy but a woman's dream of empowerment, and that makes all the difference.

It's all onscreen when we first meet the amnesiac "Vers" among the alien Kree race, though it takes a while for the full reality of her abilities to become apparent. We soon learn that she can create and project plasma blasts from her fists, that she is unusually strong, and she's reminded that the Kree gave her these powers and can take them away. Vers is plagued by dreams and insomnia, unsure of her own strength. Her response to trauma is to fight; her response to authority is to laugh. All those holes in her memories and an almost instant display of short temper mean she's immediately set apart from more caricatured "strong female characters". Her mentor among the alien Kree, Yon-Rogg (Jude Law), indulges her desire for combat but continually has to rein in her impulses.

Involved in a war between the Kree and the shapeshifting Skrull, Vers is briefly captured before pursuing the Skrull to 1990s Earth – and learning that she once had a life there. It's then a process of finding out both what happened to her and how she can reach the prize her enemy is pursuing first.

Particularly on Earth, there's no getting away from the significance of being Marvel's first solo female lead. Just as Black Panther embraced his identity as a black African, this film embraces Danvers' status as a woman, thanks to a screenplay by Geneva Robertson-Dworet and directors Anna Boden and Ryan Fleck. She is someone who has continually been told she is too emotional, not ready, not enough. The memories that have survived include men sneering at her, endless knock-backs and knock-downs, a long struggle to be taken seriously. We finally realize that she was a test pilot on Earth, because she wasn't allowed to fly combat missions, and we meet the other two women who shaped her destiny: Annette Bening's quietly encouraging "Dr Wendy Lawson" – or, as it turns out, Mar-Vell, a Kree somehow involved with Carol getting her powers – and Lashana Lynch's Maria Rambeau, her sister from another mister and closest friend and colleague.

Larson was cast after she won the Oscar for her stunning performance in *Room*, and she creates a defiant, tough and tenacious figure with just enough

Opposite Carol Danvers (Brie Larson), not officially called Captain Marvel yet, back on Earth and ready to fight.

humour and heart to avoid cliché. The humour is particularly important: on Earth, among other people who understand her jokes for the first time in her memory, she visibly relaxes. It's less a boost of confidence and more a sense of being at home as she realizes that she's not the only one who likes to poke fun at the powers that be. Key to that growth is her relationship with Samuel L. Jackson's young Nick Fury, stunningly de-aged to convince as a man who doesn't yet know everything. But she blossoms further when she reconnects with Maria and her daughter Monica (Akira Akbar), who were the centre of her emotional life on Earth.

The bad guy they eventually defeat is not quite as expected – though, on a rewatch, you'll see that all the signs are there – but their identity is not the point. While this film is not a traditional origin story and, in fact, tries hard to avoid those beats, they get to the point of showing us how Carol got her powers in the end. But, as Maria says, she was powerful long before she had the ability to shoot fire from her fists. Carol Danvers realizes that her whole life has been about getting knocked down and standing back up again. So she stands back up, stops limiting her powers and wins the day. No matter who tells her she's too weak, too emotional, not enough, she has what it takes.

Top Jude Law's Yon-Rogg, the leader of Carol's team.

Above A cat called Goose. Fans will know that this kitty matters.

Opposite, top Maria Rambeau (Lashana Lynch), Carol's ace co-pilot and partner in crime.

Opposite, bottom A stunningly de-aged Samuel L. Jackson shows us Nick Fury pre-eye-patch.

The finale is not taking down the bad guys or single-handedly destroying their ship; it's when she stops waiting for permission to do so. And that's a story in which everyone, male or female or non-binary, can find inspiration.

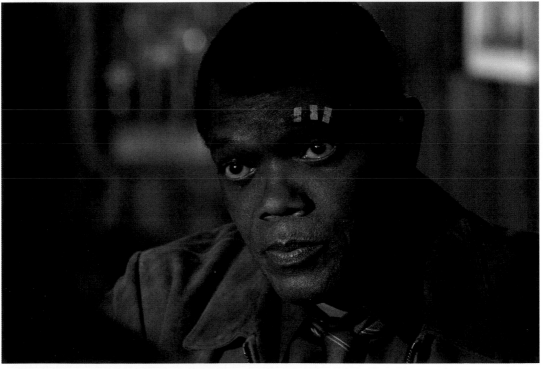

SHAZAM!

SOME WOULD CLAIM THAT ALL SUPERHERO FILMS ARE CHILDISH WISH FULFILLMENT FANTASIES, BUT IT'S A FAIR DESCRIPTION IN THE CASE OF *SHAZAM!*, WHERE A LITERAL CHILD TRANSFORMED INTO A ROUGHLY SUPERMAN-LEVEL HERO (ZACHARY LEVI). RATHER THAN RAIL AGAINST OR RUN FROM CHARGES OF IMMATURITY, HOWEVER, *SHAZAM!* EMBRACES THEM.

The film layers its central conceit with shades of *Big*, *Ghostbusters*, *Gremlins* and *Goonies*. Sticking close to the model of an 1980s Amblin film is a smart choice for the character, and it gives us the most purely fun DC movie since *Batman Returns*.

Director David F. Sandberg was previously best known for work in horror like *Light's Out*, and he treads a careful line to nail his tone here. There are scary and upsetting moments, but they're largely balanced by the sense of joy and freedom that the unhappy Billy Batson (Asher Angel) feels when he transforms into Levi's superhero after encountering the wizard Shazam (Djimon Hounsou). Billy is a foster kid so obsessed with the search for his birth family that he has always failed to consider the possibility that he might forge another. After running away to find his long-lost mother once too often, he is sent to a new group home with a gang of misfit foster siblings who might actually prove a fit – if only he'd let them.

Like *The Goonies*, the kids are a pleasantly weird bunch, from the comics-obsessed Freddie (Jack Dylan Grazer) to the extremely huggy Darla (Faithe Herman). As the resident superhero expert, it's to Freddie that Billy turns when he discovers his new power. Or rather, Levi's Shazam turns to Freddie, because there's a clear divide between the withdrawn Billy and the gleeful, daring alter-ego he gains.

Perhaps joy has always lain within Billy, dormant through the many tough days of his childhood, but we don't really get to see it until he says the magic word ("Shazam", that is) and transforms. It's a slight problem for the storytelling: almost all of Billy's happiest moments happen in his other form, so that the two halves of his personality feel a little too distinct. Still, the withdrawn Billy is slowly dragged into the light by Shazam and Freddie's friendship, discovering his powers while keeping them a secret from the adult world. But soon, of course, he must fight a baddie: Mark Strong's Thaddeus Sivana.

As with many superhero match-ups, Billy and his nemesis are one another's fun-house mirror reflection. Sivana was born with every material advantage, though like Billy he was unloved by a careless parent (John Glover). Thad is offered the power of Shazam as a child, but rejected as unworthy by the wizard. Just as Billy obsessively searched for his mother, Sivana spent his life looking for a way back, and became a vehicle for the "Seven Sins" that Billy, the eventual chosen one, must defeat. The difference is that, come the crunch, Billy choses to share power. To defeat Sivana in the final battle, he invites his foster siblings in and shares his power

Opposite Zachary Levi looking characteristically nonchalant as Shazam.

with them, allowing them to transform into similarly powerful heroes (amusingly, two of the actors who play the adult siblings, D.J. Cotrona and Adam Brody, were cast in George Miller's never-made Justice League movie, giving them a little extra resonance).

It's a well-stacked premise, but that's not the killer blow here: *Shazam!* is *funny*, really funny, with a lightness of touch and willingness to acknowledge its own absurdities that rivals *Deadpool*. A lot of that humour comes from Henry Gayden's script, but more from star Zachary Levi's gleeful take on how it feels to suddenly feel free and powerful in a world that had previously ignored your existence. His fun is infectious, and it carries us all through the

Above The sense of giddy joy that Shazam (Levi) and Freddie (Jack Dylan Grazer) exude is palpable.

Opposite, above Mark Strong plays up his dour villain persona to the max – and it works.

Opposite, below Levi nails the wide-eyed naivete of a child stuck in a superhero's body.

film's darker and scarier moments. When it comes to fantasy escapism and the sheer giddy joy of having superpowers, this hits all the spots. Not every film, after all, needs grim-dark seriousness and universe-spanning stakes, and *Shazam!* shows that there's still room for kids to have fun pretending to be Superman. Or, in this case, genuinely being his peer.

THE TV SUPERHERO TAKEOVER

NOT CONTENT WITH RULING THE BOX OFFICE, CAPED CRUSADERS OF ALL SORTS HAVE ALSO TAKEN OVER THE SMALL SCREEN AS WELL, AND STARTED BUILDING LINKS BETWEEN SHOWS. HERE'S A VERY QUICK GUIDE TO THE PRINCIPAL SHARED UNIVERSES OF THE SMALL SCREEN, IN CASE YOU NEED A FIX BETWEEN BLOCKBUSTER RELEASES.

MARVEL/ABC
AGENTS OF S.H.I.E.L.D.
AGENT CARTER
INHUMANS

The first MCU spin-off is also the most closely connected with its parent universe as S.H.I.E.L.D., led by Clark Gregg's Agent Coulson and Ming-Na's Agent May, deals with the fall-out of the bigger films. *Agent Carter*, in contrast, took things back to the earliest days of the agency and saw Hayley Atwell's Peggy Carter fight her own bosses as well as the bad guys. And *The Inhumans*, sadly, never quite took off and were sort of written out of history.

THE ARROWVERSE
ARROW
THE FLASH
SUPERGIRL
CONSTANTINE
LEGENDS OF TOMORROW

DC's small-screen shared universe is, perhaps, the most successful of the lot. It started with the relatively familiar *Arrow* – another billionaire with a dark past and cool toys – but went truly super with *The Flash*, first of all, and then *Supergirl*, both of them lighter and more cheery than their parent series. Their crossover episodes were glorious fun, though things got really confusing with the time-shenanigans of *Legends of Tomorrow* and when Constantine was retroactively added to the mix, even after his series was officially cancelled. *Arrow* finally wrapped up after eight seasons, but its universe lived on.

MARVEL/NETFLIX

DAREDEVIL
JESSICA JONES
LUKE CAGE
IRON FIST
THE PUNISHER
THE DEFENDERS

This shared universe launched with *Daredevil* and almost instantly rehabilitated the character, with a back-to-basics approach that initially ditched the uniform and the name. Similarly gritty, largely grounded, highly successful shows followed in *Jessica Jones*, *Luke Cage* and *The Punisher*, though *Iron Fist* and crossover series *The Defenders* were less well received. The shows were cancelled in late 2018 and early 2019, prior to the launch of Disney's own streaming service, but they proved that Marvel could go darker and still work.

AVENGERS: INFINITY WAR AND AVENGERS: ENDGAME

THE FIRST *AVENGERS* WAS A DARING EXPERIMENT. *AGE OF ULTRON*, FOR ALL ITS FLAWS, PROVED THAT IT WAS NO FLASH IN THE PAN. BUT THE TWO-PART WHAMMY THAT IS *INFINITY WAR* AND *ENDGAME* ARE AN ACHIEVEMENT ON A DIFFERENT SCALE.

The Marvel universe had expanded exponentially since 2012, and the ambition of its crossover events had to rise accordingly. So this two-part epic assembles perhaps the biggest A-list cast ever, and then uses it to tell a story that continually goes against the superhero grain – including the most devastating defeat of blockbuster history.

Marvel established this show's villain, Thanos (Josh Brolin), way back in the post-credit sting to *Avengers*. But he remained a peripheral figure until *Infinity War*. Directors Joe and Anthony Russo, with screenwriters

Christopher Marcus and Stephen McFeely, were coming off the two best *Captain America* movies and decided to stick with what worked: moral complexity, sticky ethical quandaries and an opponent who might, maybe, have a point. Despite all the stars at their disposal, big CG Thanos is therefore the protagonist

Opposite The *Infinity War* poster artwork rams home just how broad and deep the MCU has become.

Below This fantastic publicity shot for *Infinity War* is a tissue of lies, but it still looks cool.

Avengers have five long years to fully appreciate the magnitude of their failures. How they deal with that loss is instructive: a super-powered representation of the five stages of grief. Cap and Black Widow keep doing what they can to help people as if nothing has changed; Thor retreats from the world into a pit of despair and alcohol, tormented by how he could have acted differently; Tony finally learns to appreciate the little things. And Hawkeye takes his furious revenge out on every scumbag who survived the moment that his family did not. They are universally guilt-plagued, traumatized and unsure of themselves. That's when a rat (the unsung hero of *Endgame*) trips a switch and accidentally brings Ant-Man back from the Quantum Realm, opening the possibility of time travel and the chance to put right what Thanos made wrong. This kick-starts the "time heist" middle act of the film, a largely joyous romp through *Avengers* history that spins wittily off previous films.

This section goes a long way in helping us overlook *Thor: The Dark World*'s shortcomings, thanks to a moving cameo from Rene Russo as his mum, Frigga, and the reappearance of Mjolnir to remind Thor of his worth. Tony finally wraps up his father

issues thanks to a time-travelling catch-up, and Cap glimpses Peggy after years apart. As an entire era of *Avengers* on-screen history is wrapped up here, we can rest assured that our heroes will leave in a healthier emotional state than they began it. That even applies to moments of the film that replay missions we've seen before. When someone must die to acquire the Soul Stone, it's bosom buddies Black Widow and Hawkeye battling to sacrifice themselves and save the other, where Thanos simply murdered his daughter as she struggled for life. "We don't trade lives," claimed Steve Rogers in *Infinity War*, but that's not quite right. Each Avenger is each willing to trade his or her own life; they just won't countenance trading anyone else's. "Whatever it takes," to undo Thanos' act and save the world.

That's the heroism we expect, and in *Endgame* we finally get the (mostly) happy ending we expect. But the film is still remarkable in its commitment to grief and trauma. With 21 films behind it, we care about these characters, and we're more engaged with their struggles than we would be in any standalone film. We can read a world of regret and weight into tiny pauses and things unsaid: this shared cinematic

universe experiment pays off in every scene. We laugh when Rocket eyes Bucky's arm; we delight at the bickering between the Guardians and Iron Man; we understand that Peter Parker's idea of an "old" movie may be very different to the rest of the gang. Almost every previous film – even *The Incredible Hulk* – gets a nod here, and a keen-eyed fan can take endless pleasure in spotting the repeated poses, echoed lines and resurrected stories. Howard the Duck is even visible in the background of one shot.

Amid all the trauma, arguing, and failure, there is glorious satisfaction. Cap picks up Mjolnir in his hour of need, proving himself worthy to wield the power of Thor as we all suspected. Thor 'powers up' Iron Man for a massive strike on Thanos. Scott Lang expands into Giant Man to save Hulk, War Machine and Rocket. And all that pales next to the return of the previously dusted heroes, heralded by Sam Wilson's crackled "On your left". That call-back to *The Winter Soldier* adds to the euphoria of an already near-overwhelming moment. Call it fan service if you like, but the most effective of these scenes link back to stories and character traits set up years ago, so that it rarely feels cheap. And the

action in scale and content is impeccable, treating us to the greatest comic-book splash pages ever put onscreen. In one, Cap stands alone against an army in the dying light of the sun. In another the Avengers, finally assembled, face a suddenly shaken Thanos. The warlord has never been truly challenged before. He's right to worry.

True to its name, *Endgame* brings three phases and one era of Marvel to a true end. Tony Stark finally makes the "sacrifice play" that Cap once said was beyond him; Steve Rogers finally lives the life that always seemed out of his reach; Natasha Romanov definitively clears any hint of red from her ledger. The end is bittersweet, but it leaves us with a feeling of completeness and finality rare in the superhero sphere – and with many heroes still on the field to form a New Avengers in the future. If *Infinity War* is a victory lap for the 18 films before it, *Endgame* is the race won again, this time backwards and in heels.

Above *Endgame* sees Robert Downey Jr and Chris Evans take centre stage – for the last time?

Opposite It's the hope that kills: the remaining Avengers prepare to pull off a time heist.

THE LEGACY OF STAN LEE

OR, WHY DID THAT ONE GUY KEEP TURNING UP IN ALL MY FAVOURITE MOVIES?

There is no one in the history of comics quite like Stan Lee. He started working in comics at 17, and was appointed editor of what became *Marvel* in 1941 before he even turned 20. Aside from a brief stint working on wartime propaganda, he would hold that position for over 30 years and shape generations of comics readers.

However, mere longevity is not how Lee became an icon. By 1960, he considered quitting *Marvel* in search of fresh challenges. But his wife, Joan, with whom he would spend 70 years, suggested that he give it one last chance and really swing for the fences this time. There followed a four-year inspiration binge during which Lee co-created the X-Men, the Hulk, the Fantastic Four and Spider-Man: a creative streak that few have paralleled in any artform. Working with hugely important creators such as Jack Kirby and Steve Ditko, and at the head of an army of talented writers and artists, Lee established the typical Marvel heroes. They were underdogs, often social rejects and always strangely relatable, however cosmic their powers.

Spider-Man is a typical example. His powers made his life harder, not easier, and yet he remained eternally optimistic and as ready with a quip as a kick when fighting bad guys. Or consider X-Men, a marginalized group of individuals who fought to protect the ordinary people who fear them. All these heroes are imbued with Lee's optimism and genial good nature, and a passion for social justice that he made explicit in his editor's letters.

Of course, the fans also love Lee's film work. In 1981, in the wake of Superman's big-screen success, Lee moved to Hollywood to try to launch Marvel

in movies. Despite some very cheap, very bad adaptations early on, Lee's tireless cheerleading kept Marvel in the public mind and eventually led to the successes of *Blade*, *X-Men*, *Spider-Man* and the Marvel Cinematic Universe. A Lee cameo became a tradition in almost all the films that followed (he missed *X2*), and such a running gag that he even lampooned himself in arch-rival DC's *Teen Titans Go! to the Movies*.

Lee died late in 2018 at the age of 95, shortly after his wife. He left behind a few final cameos, which made for emotional viewing, and a deep bench of characters with an indefatigable spirit of hope and a determination to do the right thing. And, along the way, he made "true believers" of us all.